Minecraft® Redstone

FOR DUMMIES®
A Wiley Brand

Portable Edition

by Jacob Cordeiro

D1497693

FOR DUMMIES®
A Wiley Brand

Minecraft® Redstone For Dummies®, Portable Edition

Published by **John Wiley & Sons, Inc.,** 111 River Street, Hoboken, NJ 07030-5774, www.wiley.com

Copyright © 2015 by John Wiley & Sons, Inc., Hoboken, New Jersey

Published simultaneously in Canada

No part of this publication may be reproduced, stored in a retrieval system or transmitted in any form or by any means, electronic, mechanical, photocopying, recording, scanning or otherwise, except as permitted under Sections 107 or 108 of the 1976 United States Copyright Act, without either the prior written permission of the Publisher. Requests to the Publisher for permission should be addressed to the Permissions Department, John Wiley & Sons, Inc., 111 River Street, Hoboken, NJ 07030, (201) 748-6011, fax (201) 748-6008, or online at http://www.wiley.com/go/permissions.

Trademarks: Wiley, For Dummies, the Dummies Man logo, Dummies.com, Making Everything Easier, and related trade dress are trademarks or registered trademarks of John Wiley & Sons, Inc. and/or its affiliates in the United States and other countries, and may not be used without written permission. Minecraft is a registered trademark of Notch Development. All other trademarks are the property of their respective owners. John Wiley & Sons, Inc. is not associated with any product or vendor mentioned in this book.

LIMIT OF LIABILITY/DISCLAIMER OF WARRANTY: THE PUBLISHER AND THE AUTHOR MAKE NO REPRESENTATIONS OR WARRANTIES WITH RESPECT TO THE ACCURACY OR COMPLETE-NESS OF THE CONTENTS OF THIS WORK AND SPECIFICALLY DISCLAIM ALL WARRANTIES, INCLUDING WITHOUT LIMITATION WARRANTIES OF FITNESS FOR A PARTICULAR PURPOSE. NO WARRANTY MAY BE CREATED OR EXTENDED BY SALES OR PROMOTIONAL MATERIALS. THE ADVICE AND STRATEGIES CONTAINED HEREIN MAY NOT BE SUITABLE FOR EVERY SITU-ATION. THIS WORK IS SOLD WITH THE UNDERSTANDING THAT THE PUBLISHER IS NOT ENGAGED IN RENDERING LEGAL, ACCOUNTING, OR OTHER PROFESSIONAL SERVICES. IF PRO-FESSIONAL ASSISTANCE IS REQUIRED, THE SERVICES OF A COMPETENT PROFESSIONAL PERSON SHOULD BE SOUGHT. NEITHER THE PUBLISHER NOR THE AUTHOR SHALL BE LIABLE FOR DAMAGES ARISING HEREFROM. THE FACT THAT AN ORGANIZATION OR WEBSITE IS REFERRED TO IN THIS WORK AS A CITATION AND/OR A POTENTIAL SOURCE OF FURTHER INFORMATION DOES NOT MEAN THAT THE AUTHOR OR THE PUBLISHER ENDORSES THE INFORMATION THE ORGANIZATION OR WEBSITE MAY PROVIDE OR RECOMMENDATIONS IT MAY MAKE. FURTHER, READERS SHOULD BE AWARE THAT INTERNET WEBSITES LISTED IN THIS WORK MAY HAVE CHANGED OR DISAPPEARED BETWEEN WHEN THIS WORK WAS WRIT-TEN AND WHEN IT IS READ.

For general information on our other products and services, please contact our Customer Care Department within the U.S. at 877-762-2974, outside the U.S. at 317-572-3993, or fax 317-572-4002. For technical support, please visit www.wiley.com/techsupport.

Wiley publishes in a variety of print and electronic formats and by print-on-demand. Some material included with standard print versions of this book may not be included in e-books or in print-on-demand. If this book refers to media such as a CD or DVD that is not included in the version you purchased, you may download this material at http://booksupport.wiley.com. For more information about Wiley products, visit www.wiley.com.

Library of Congress Control Number: 2014941047

ISBN 978-1-118-96830-7 (pbk); ISBN 978-1-118-96833-8 (ebk); ISBN 978-1-118-96832-1

Manufactured in Great Britain by Bell and Bain Ltd, Glasgow

10 9 8 7 6 5 4 3 2 1

Table of Contents

Introduction

Much of the appeal of Minecraft lies in how much you can do with it — you can move most blocks and entities however you want, and you can build lots of different items to a gigantic scale. However, the power of *redstone* takes this concept further — using this component of Minecraft, you can program, automate, and creatively reconstruct your world. *Minecraft Redstone For Dummies,* Portable Edition, teaches you how to use special blocks and items to devise circuits, programs, machines, and other incredible devices from within this versatile video game. In this book, you can find out about everything from electrical engineering to computer programming in a fun, interesting environment.

Redstone refers to various blocks that can be powered or unpowered with a sort of electric charge — they can be powered by certain sources, and they can power other items in turn. Following concepts from circuitry and electronics, this system lets you hook up devices and mechanisms to simple or complex arrangements for many different results. I also discuss other facets of Minecraft programming, such as pistons and physical machines, customized entities and items, and the versatile command block.

 Version 1.8 of Minecraft, the last update covered by this book, makes some fundamental changes to the game in order to make certain parts of redstone engineering more versatile and accessible. Future versions of the game probably won't change how the content explained in this book works.

About This Book

In this book, you can read about everything from the purpose of redstone to the individual functions of redstone components to the tools for building elaborate computers.

Minecraft players who are new to redstone can use this book to understand this deep but rewarding topic and start using it in the game, and experienced players can use the book as a helpful handbook for recalling techniques and concepts. This book doesn't deal with any Minecraft *mods* (programs that add extra content to the game), but if you read some of the chapters about command blocks, you can see how to use tools that essentially let you program mods from inside the game.

Because many mechanisms that I describe in this book consist of small collections of blocks, they will inevitably resemble those designed by others. Any such resemblance is unintentional — I know I've drawn inspiration from many other users while learning the concepts of redstone myself.

Foolish Assumptions

In this book, I assume that you have at least a basic knowledge of how to play Minecraft, though you don't need to know anything about redstone or programming. I also assume that the following statements about you are true:

- You have a computer, and you know how to use it.
- You have a working copy of Minecraft, and you know how to
  - Move around the world.
  - Place, destroy, and manipulate blocks.
  - Obtain items in Creative mode.
  - Use the Chat menu.

Icons Used in This Book

Certain useful paragraphs in this book are marked with special icons in the margins. The icons and their purposes are described in this section:

This icon points out useful tips that may help you improve your techniques.

I recommend reading the information next to these icons if you're only skimming the book — they call attention to information that you should remember while working with redstone.

Definitely read the paragraphs marked by the Warning icon. This icon warns you about things you should avoid when working with redstone, from common mistakes to total game-crashers.

You can generally skip this type of information, if you want, because it's quite technical. However, you may find it interesting to read and learn about.

Where to Go from Here

If you're inexperienced or completely new to the concept of redstone, you will find the earliest chapters quite helpful, as well as Chapter 7, which is an introduction to the command block. Experienced players can find specific advice by skimming this book, and more advanced concepts are covered in Chapters 5, 8, and 9.

Occasionally, *For Dummies* technology books are updated. If this book has technical updates, they'll be posted at www. dummies.com/go/minecraftredstoneupdates.

1

Introducing Redstone

*T*he world of the game Minecraft is appealing in its infiniteness. In a game where every piece of the world can be destroyed, modified, and rearranged, the possibilities are limitless for how you can work, construct, and venture to make the world your own. This feature is particularly visible in the study of a few choice blocks and items that can function together to form machines of enormous size and scale. The tools, and the science behind these machines, are referred to as redstone.

This chapter introduces you to the basic structure and possibilities of redstone machines.

Exploring Redstone Basics

Redstone is a dust that you can find underground and use like wiring. Redstone can connect power suppliers (such as levers and buttons) to devices (such as doors and pistons), using the power suppliers to activate the devices from any distance.

You can use redstone to build an automatic door, a light switch, or a trap for the monsters that haunt your Minecraft world. For example, Figure 1-1 shows how a Minecraft player added a redstone circuit to his house so that he can turn on all the lights on the walls with the flip of a lever. Though these tricks are useful for improving your Minecraft experience, the full extent of redstone's possibilities is much more expansive.

Redstone dust

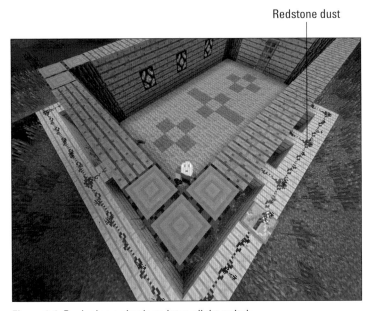

Figure 1-1: Designing a simple redstone light switch.

Redstone technology is often used to build *functions* — machines that convert input (such as flipping a lever or tripping a tripwire) into output (such as activating TNT or moving blocks around). Simply connecting the input to the output with redstone dust is sufficient to design a function. However, you can create more complex functions with the tools I introduce in Chapter 2. For example, you may want your output to activate only if two buttons are pressed at the same time.

Essentially, redstone gives you the tools to turn any input into any output. This subject is extremely powerful — after all, the computer on which you play Minecraft is simply a collection of many, many functions. And people *have* built computers in Minecraft, designed for various features and functions. Chapter 5 describes the study of combining functions into interesting creations.

Understanding How Redstone Works

Redstone functions on the same principles as logic and computer science. The difference is that, rather than have lines of code or wires and resistors, you have physical blocks arranged in a virtual world. The idea behind redstone devices is that they can be either on or off — powered or unpowered — depending on what is happening to them.

Most redstone components, including the ever-present redstone dust, are unpowered until they're charged by other redstone components or inputs such as levers. Throughout this book, the presence of power within a redstone circuit is referred to as a redstone *charge* or redstone *current.* (In real-life circuits, these terms mean different things, but redstone power could pass for either.) Though the basic redstone dust can be used in many ways to link components, other blocks — such as redstone torches, redstone repeaters, and redstone comparators, all described in Chapter 2 — can invert, delay, and modify the current. That's where the real fun happens.

Figure 1-2 shows a redstone *circuit* (an arrangement that produces a specific effect), consisting of many different components. Depending on the position of the levers at the bottom of the figure, the redstone current is passed among the various sections of the machine, working together to perform the function designed by the builder.

Many of the figures throughout this book look like Figure 1-2, with the components of the machine spread out clearly. Others are compact and concise. This book therefore tries to show you designs that are easier to break apart and understand, in addition to the efficient and elegant creations that you may see in your future constructive journeys.

Figure 1-2: A redstone machine in multiple parts.

Discovering the Applications of Redstone

Using redstone allows for plenty of possibilities, but can it do anything other than use items to activate other items? Fortunately, Minecraft provides a wealth of challenges and opportunities to which you can apply the concepts from this book:

- **Combination locks:** This is a popular first project for redstone engineers who are transitioning from the basics of design to the theory of it. A combination lock activates the output only when a collection of levers is set to a particular arrangement.

- **Automatic machines:** By using pistons, dispensers, and other devices, you can build machines that harvest crops, brew potions, manage minecarts, or perform basic tasks for you. By having machines do some of your work, you can design a more efficient Minecraft world, gathering more resources faster.

- **Dynamic structures:** Use pistons to raise bridges, move walls, or push arrangements together. Create waterfalls that can be controlled with floodgates, automatic doors, or elaborate lighting systems — anything in your world can be manipulated with redstone. Take advantage of it!

- **Traps and choreographed events:** Many players enjoy first building adventure-style worlds run by redstone and then sending the worlds to other players for them to try out. Whether you're building a challenge for another player or you want a brilliant, new way to punish trespassers, you can use redstone to guide the people in your world.

- **World management:** Redstone can control the form and function of the world, especially with the cheats-only command block. You can set the rules of the world, manage a scoreboard, fill huge areas with blocks, copy buildings, or summon giant slimes riding bats across the sky, for example. See Chapter 7 for more on the command block.

- **Minigames:** Games follow input-output structures as well — Minecraft players have designed many excellent redstone-powered games for other players to try. See Chapter 10 for more on this topic.

- **Theoretical machines:** Sometimes a machine doesn't have a purpose — an interesting algorithm or component can have value in itself. Many players use Creative mode just to build elegant, innovative, and aesthetic machines.

You can apply redstone in many more ways in either Survival mode or Creative mode. You can find some of them by reading further in this book or by innovating on your own.

2

Getting Started with Redstone Programming

*U*nderstanding how redstone works can be difficult because few games allow you to program whatever you want from raw ingredients. This chapter helps you program your first basic machines (from linking levers and doors to building simple locks) with the power of redstone dust. I also describe the fundamentals of using redstone throughout Chapters 3 and 4, but this chapter is a good starting point for new players.

Gathering Redstone Dust

In Creative mode in Minecraft, redstone supplies are freely available. However, if you're playing Minecraft in Survival mode, you need to gather the materials necessary to build your circuit. The most fundamental tool you need is the *redstone dust* item. Redstone dust can be not only used raw as a simple machine but also crafted into many other redstone-based devices.

To get redstone dust, you need to mine *redstone ore*. In Figure 2-1, redstone ore is the stone with little chunks of red material embedded in the side.

Redstone ore

Figure 2-1: Finding a vein of redstone ore.

You have to mine deep to find redstone ore blocks — 16 blocks from the bottom of the world. In other words, your character's y-coordinate must be 16 at most, which you can check by pressing F3. However, at the correct depth, redstone ore is relatively common. In addition, every time you mine this item, you obtain at least four piles of redstone dust (as long as you use a pickaxe made from iron or diamond). With some concentrated effort, you can have mounds of redstone in no time.

Laying Out Redstone Dust

Redstone dust is the item used to craft most other redstone devices, and it's often the most useful tool you can have when designing machines. To place a lump of redstone dust, right-click the ground to place it there (or press the Use Item button if you changed it from the default). When you place redstone dust in a trail along the ground, it acts like a wire. In its default state, the redstone wire is uncharged.

A device such as a lever, tripwire, button, or pressure plate can *power* the redstone. The powder then begins to glow red and transmit power, activating connected devices such as electric lamps or explosives. Figure 2-2 shows a simple redstone device, in which a pressure plate is connected to three lamps with a cross of redstone dust. The redstone is activated in the figure because a player is standing on the pressure plate. (See Chapter 3 for more on pressure plates.)

Redstone dust   Powered lamp

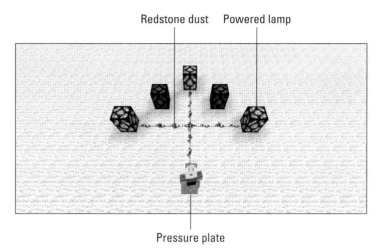

Pressure plate

Figure 2-2: The two darkened redstone lamps aren't turned on, because they aren't adjacent to a powered object.

As you can see in the figure, redstone dust can bend, split, and travel in all directions. It does these things automatically when you place it: When you put redstone dust in multiple adjacent squares, the pieces of dust connect to each other. To create the arrangement shown in the figure, place redstone dust on each square of the cross.

You cannot place most redstone items on transparent blocks such as glass, or on blocks that are a different shape than the standard meter cube (such as fences, beds, or slabs). Some mechanical items, such as pressure plates, can be placed on fences and the like, but usually for the sake of creating pretty furniture.

In the following sections, I explain the different properties of redstone dust.

Carrying a charge

Redstone dust can travel in all the intuitive ways, but current can also be transferred in some interesting ways. Figure 2-3 shows an interesting property of redstone dust: It can run up and down the sides of blocks. If one piece of redstone, therefore, is one block higher or lower than another, adjacent piece of redstone, they still connect.

Redstone cannot travel up more than one block at a time, as shown in the redstone trail on the left side of the figure.

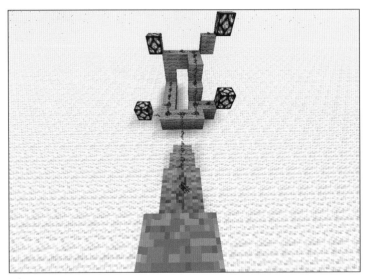

Figure 2-3: The trail of redstone dust snakes up and down to power all lamps.

The connections between adjacent pieces of redstone always form automatically, unless you place a solid block in the way. This feature is useful for making three-dimensional designs — you can build ramps to move your redstone trails up and down.

The concepts of linking up redstone in this section are the basics of using redstone dust, but you can use these principles to accomplish all sorts of tasks. Figure 2-4 shows a few examples of transporting and managing redstone current. Rather than use pressure plates to power the redstone (refer to Figures 2-2 and 2-3), I used the bright red *redstone blocks,* which provide continuous power. (See the section "Redstone blocks," later in this chapter.)

Redstone block

Figure 2-4: Carrying charge from the redstone blocks to the redstone lamps.

Measuring redstone strength

You may have noticed that redstone dust grows dimmer as it gets farther from its power source. The reason is that redstone dust can extend only 15 blocks away from its origin before it dies out, making it unable to power objects.

Redstone dust can take different levels of charge, from 0 (uncharged) to 15 (fully charged). This property obeys the following rules:

- **The charge of a piece of redstone dust is one unit less than the strongest adjacent charge.** For example, if one piece of dust is charged to 9, and another is charged to 6, a piece between them would have a charge of $9 - 1 = 8$.

- **All power-producing items other than redstone dust have a charge of 16 when active.** Any dust connected to this charge, therefore, has a charge of 15. Solid, non-redstone blocks and redstone comparators (described in the later sections "Applying powered blocks" and "Redstone comparators") are the only power producers that are exceptions — when active, they don't always carry a charge of 16, because they take the same level of charge as their inputs.

✓ **If a piece of redstone dust changes its charge, every connected piece of redstone dust does so at the same time.** You will therefore never observe two adjacent pieces of redstone dust with substantially different charges. However, other redstone devices take a short time to update. Fortunately, this length of time is consistent and measurable, so you can exploit it to make timed and choreographed circuits.

The fact that redstone dust can't travel more than 15 blocks can be a major limitation, but there are many ways to both counteract and exploit it, as described in later sections of this chapter. Just be sure that you don't make the redstone dust travel so far that the strength of the current runs out.

Connecting machines

The arrangements of redstone dust shown in Figures 2-2, 2-3, and 2-4 have been used for a particular purpose: to bring an electric current from a power source (a pressure plate or redstone block) to a mechanism (a redstone lamp). Keep in mind that you cannot simply place redstone adjacent to a mechanism and expect the mechanism to turn on. For example, some of the lamps shown in Figure 2-5 are unpowered, even though they're adjacent to redstone. The reason is that the line of redstone must be facing the mechanism for it to connect properly.

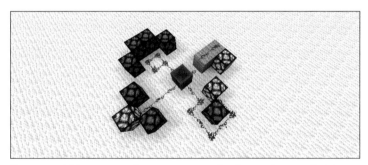

Figure 2-5: All lamps are adjacent to powered redstone, but not all of them turn on.

If the redstone dust forms lines or corners, they must face toward the mechanism. For example, a line of redstone that moves from north to south only powers mechanisms to the north and to the south. A dot of redstone (which is connected to nothing) powers mechanisms all around it.

This rule about facing toward the mechanism isn't as restrictive as you might think. Note that the redstone lamp next to the blue block shown in Figure 2-5 is turned on. Basically, powered redstone dust may not power everything around it, though the block it rests on does. The lamp is being powered through one of the blue blocks. This concept is part of an interesting rule that I describe in more detail in Chapter 4.

Crafting and Implementing Redstone Items

Redstone dust isn't the only mechanism you can use to carry and manipulate current. The following sections show you how to craft and implement other redstone-based items: redstone torches, redstone repeaters, redstone comparators, and redstone blocks.

Redstone torches

Redstone torches are useful tools for making more complex machines. They're also cheap, costing only a lump of redstone dust and a stick, as shown in Figure 2-6. The simplest use for a redstone torch is as a constant source of power. After you place it in your world, it immediately begins glowing with energy.

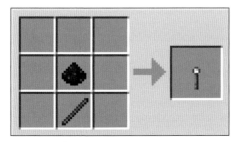

Figure 2-6: Crafting a redstone torch.

Redstone torches charge everything next to them. In addition, if a redstone torch has a solid block directly above it, anything adjacent to that block is powered. Figure 2-7 shows a single redstone torch that powers all the redstone dust and lamps in the arrangement.

Figure 2-7: The redstone torch powers nearby redstone dust, which carries charge to the lamps.

You must place a redstone torch on the top (refer to Figure 2-7) or side of a block. If the block under the torch in the figure is destroyed, the torch is destroyed as well.

Redstone torches never burn out on their own, but you can turn them off by powering the blocks they're placed on. If you provide redstone power to the block that the torch is attached to — for example, the blue wool block shown in Figure 2-8 — the torch turns off and no longer functions. When the connected block is no longer powered, the torch turns on again.

You can charge a block in one of several ways. Here are two examples:

  ✔ Run powered redstone dust directly into the block (refer to Figure 2-8) or over it.

  ✔ Place a redstone torch directly under the block, or place a *redstone repeater* or *redstone comparator* next to the block. (These tools are described in the later sections "Redstone repeaters" and "Redstone comparators.")

Figure 2-8: The powered redstone torch is charging the blue wool, which deactivates the other torches.

The precise rules for powering blocks are provided in the later section "Powering Blocks."

You can build many machines using only redstone dust, redstone torches, and player-controlled devices such as levers and pressure plates. Redstone torches represent information (because they can take either the On or Off position), and redstone dust carries input to output.

Figure 2-9 shows a complex example. Don't worry if you don't yet understand it — it's intended only to show how these simple components can create interesting and practical machines. The machine is a programmable, 5-bit combination tester, made up of redstone dust, redstone torches, and blocks. The redstone lamp turns on if (and only if) the five levers at the top of the device are set in the same arrangement as the bottom five. For example, if the levers at the top are placed up-down-up-up-down, the levers at the bottom must have the same values in the same order.

This popular machine is used for combination locks, riddles, and simple games — and though many users apply the special devices described later in this chapter, such as redstone repeaters and redstone comparators, all this machine needs is dust, torches, and blocks. The redstone dust connects and transfers power while interacting with carefully placed torches, turning complex input into simple output.

Figure 2-9: You see, from top to bottom, the front view, back view, and side view of the machine.

Turning simple objects into complex machines can be a challenging task, but it helps to keep these tips in mind when using redstone torches in your circuit:

- ✔ **Consider the "status" of each portion of a circuit: whether it is powered or unpowered.** Often in a large circuit, portions of it are unpowered and other portions are powered. Because unpowered redstone doesn't turn off redstone torches, a single piece of redstone can cause two different effects, depending on its state.

- ✔ **Redstone torches don't simply charge redstone — they manipulate it.** Recall the basic function of the redstone torch: It powers every mechanism adjacent to it, unless something is powering the block it connects to. In this way, torches represent functions that produce output (power or no power) depending on input (whether the block is being powered). This property makes torches extremely valuable when building *gates,* which are fundamental machines that I describe in Chapter 5.

- ✔ **Torches "flip" current.** If a torch receives power as input, it outputs no power; however, if it receives no power as input, it outputs power. When you see a torch as part of a circuit, you know that it will output the opposite of whatever goes into it.

It takes a short bit of time for a torch to turn off or on. A redstone device with many components may even take a little while to process when you pull the switch. However, you can also chain together redstone torches to make a timer and use them to extend redstone current past the maximum 15 blocks. It's the most resource-efficient way to extend current, though you can also use an interesting item known as the redstone repeater, as I describe next.

Redstone repeaters

The relationship between redstone dust and redstone torches is elegant in its simplicity because you can make so many different machines by simply combining these two items with blocks — however, *redstone repeaters* make the work a lot easier.

Repeaters are small and versatile and highly necessary for efficient and compact designs, but they're also a bit more difficult to craft than simple redstone items. A single repeater requires the following items (see Figure 2-10):

⌐ Two redstone torches

⌐ A lump of redstone dust

⌐ Three blocks of smooth stone (obtained by smelting cobblestone blocks in a furnace)

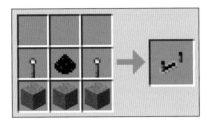

Figure 2-10: Crafting a redstone repeater.

A *redstone repeater,* as shown in Figure 2-11, is a gray panel that can be placed on most standard blocks. Repeaters, unlike dust and torches, cannot be powered from any side: They can be charged only from the back, and they can transfer charge only to the front.

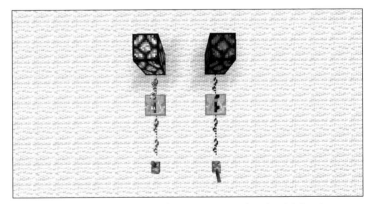

Figure 2-11: An active (on the left) and an inactive (on the right) redstone repeater.

The triangular indentation on top indicates the direction of the charge; power is translated from the wide end of the triangle to the tip. When you place a repeater, the output end faces away from you.

The repeater also contains two small redstone torches on its top. The first torch is at the vertex of the triangle, and the second is placed on a slider behind it. You can adjust the second torch's position on the slider by using the Use Item button (which is, by default, the right mouse button).

The farther apart the two torches are, the longer it takes for the repeater to update its output when the input changes. This delay time can be one, two, three, or four times that of a normal redstone torch. Basically, repeaters take the input behind them, delay for a moment, and then copy the input in front.

Exploring applications of the redstone repeater

A few properties of redstone repeaters make them individually useful:

- **Repeaters are adjustable timers.** For example, if one branch of a circuit is slightly faster than another, you can put in a repeater to ensure that the branches are aligned. You can also string together lots of repeaters to delay a circuit for a longer period.

- **Repeaters fit well with other mechanisms.** Redstone dust can be tricky, because it automatically connects with mechanisms around it. Repeaters don't have this problem: Because repeaters have only one way to receive and produce power, they function only when you want them to.

- **Repeaters are powerful.** Current can travel 15 blocks after leaving a repeater. If you want to extend a wire of redstone, therefore, all you have to do is place repeaters at 15-block intervals for the wire to run quickly and smoothly. In addition, if a powered repeater faces a solid block directly adjacent to it, all mechanisms adjacent to that block are powered. This feature makes the repeater the simplest way to power blocks, as described in the later section "Powering Blocks."

Figure 2-12 shows three simple ways that you can apply redstone repeaters in a circuit. From left to right, the figure shows a repeater-based timer, a width of current that travels in a loop, and a little example of how compact repeater-based designs can become.

Figure 2-12: Applying redstone repeaters in a circuit.

Locking redstone repeaters

The redstone repeater also has an interesting secondary function, which requires two repeaters to accomplish. If you place a redstone repeater in such a way that it connects directly into the side of an adjacent repeater, you can power the first repeater to *lock* the second.

A locked repeater cannot change its state. Regardless of input, a powered, locked repeater stays powered, and an unpowered locked repeater stays unpowered, until the repeater is unlocked — it unlocks automatically when the locking repeater is no longer powered.

In Figure 2-13, each north-facing repeater was set to its current state and then locked, thus acting regardless of its input. The gray bar across a repeater indicates that it's locked.

The ability to lock redstone repeaters is useful for making circuits that can be halted with a shutoff switch — just put a repeater at the end and add a lever that locks it when activated. Of course, like all redstone properties, it can be applied in many other ways. For example, a locked repeater's charge cannot be tampered with unless the locking device is shut off first, allowing you to store data and build locks.

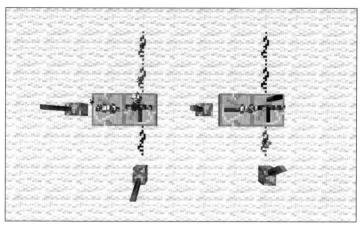

Figure 2-13: This is what locked repeater setups look like.

Redstone comparators

 The tricky device known as a *redstone comparator* has many different properties and capabilities. It compares two different redstone currents — one is behind the comparator, and one is to the side. The comparator has two settings: One passes on the back current only if it exceeds the side current; another takes the difference of the two currents' strength. This property can be difficult to understand right away, so in the rest of this section, I provide some useful examples to help you get started.

The redstone comparator looks a lot like the redstone repeater (described in the preceding section), and it can be placed in the same way: It has a front for output and a back for input, and it can only be placed on most solid blocks. However, rather than have a torch on a slider in the back, it has two torches in the back corners. (Figure 2-14 shows how to craft a redstone comparator.)

Understanding the essential comparator function

The simplest property of a redstone comparator is that, unlike the redstone repeater, the charge going in is as strong as the charge coming out. For example, if redstone dust travels 8 blocks into a comparator, the output can travel another 7 blocks before reaching the 15-block limit.

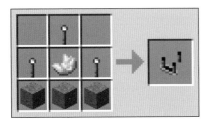

Figure 2-14: Crafting a redstone comparator.

 When working with redstone comparators, charge is vital. You may recall that redstone dust has a lower charge the farther it gets from a power source. The value of this charge affects how comparators function.

When a powered redstone dust, repeater, or comparator is directed into the *side* of a comparator, the comparator's output is affected. However, the effect depends on the comparator's setting. As with the redstone repeater, you can press the Use Item button (which is, by default, the right mouse button) to change the comparator's settings. This action toggles the setting of the torch in front of the capacitor between On and Off, as shown in Figure 2-15.

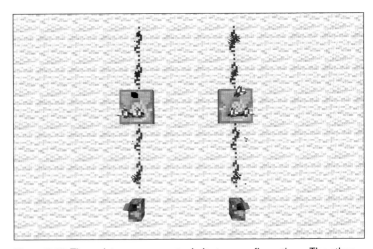

Figure 2-15: The redstone comparator in its two configurations. The other two torches turn on when the comparator is powered.

The redstone comparator has one property that functions regardless of the comparator's setting: It doesn't provide an output if the charge going into the side is stronger than the charge going into the back. For example, if redstone dust reaches both the side and back of a comparator but the path to the side is shorter, the comparator's output always has a charge of 0. However, when the side charge is less than or equal to the back charge, two things can happen:

✔ **If the comparator's front torch is in the Off position,** the output has the same charge as the input. Simple, right?

✔ **If the comparator's front torch is in the On position,** the output's charge is equal to the input charge *minus* the charge going into the side. For example, if the charge on the side is 8 and the charge on the back is 11, the output has a charge of 11–8 = 3.

This concept has many different applications. You can compare two numbers by connecting charges to the back and side of a comparator. You can use them to create specific levels of charge and then manipulate and combine them to produce the results you want. For example, Figure 2-16 shows three examples of how comparators might function. From left to right, the figure shows a simple lock, a machine that produces a charge of 1, and a setup that rapidly changes between powered and unpowered.

Figure 2-16: Several different applications for comparators.

Using comparators with containers

The comparator has another useful function, which makes it especially practical. If you place a comparator next to any container (such as a chest or a dispenser) so that the container is behind the comparator, a signal is produced proportional to how full the container is.

For example, a full container provides a charge of 16 to connected comparators, and a container with a small number of items (but not 0) produces a charge of 1. The other charges are spaced evenly throughout — thus, if a chest (which has 27 slots) contains seven swords, it produces 7/27 of a full charge.

However, different items are treated differently, storage-wise. Recall that most items can be placed in stacks of 64; in other words, 64 units of the same block can be put into a single slot of a chest. Items such as swords, meanwhile, completely fill whichever slot they occupy. For example, if you put, say, 32 diamonds into a chest (half of a maximum stack), the comparator acts as though the slot is only half full.

You can use this property in many different ways, from comparing the contents of chests to manipulating objects such as hoppers. I discuss these applications more fully in Chapter 3.

Redstone blocks

 A *redstone block* powers everything around it and cannot be turned off. As with other mineral blocks in the game, you can craft a redstone block with nine lumps of redstone dust, as shown in Figure 2-17. The redstone block is surprisingly simple to implement — just place one next to whatever item you want to power.

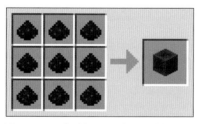

Figure 2-17: Crafting a redstone block.

You must still consider the properties of the mechanisms you want to power. For example, a redstone block doesn't power a redstone repeater unless the repeater is facing away from it.

The main appeal of the redstone block is that it is, for all intents and purposes, a block. It is therefore solid, it can be placed anywhere, and it can even be pushed and pulled while still holding a charge. These qualities make it a popular complement to the block-pushing piston: By moving a redstone block between different parts of a circuit, you can change which part of the circuit is being powered. (See Chapter 3 for more on pistons.)

Figure 2-18 shows a few examples of redstone blocks in action. The rightmost machine pushes the redstone block back and forth between two pistons. It's also governed by the same block.

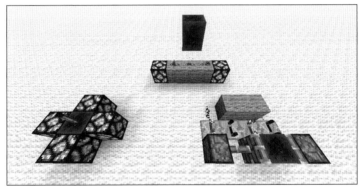

Figure 2-18: Some applications of the redstone block.

Redstone blocks, unlike other tools in this chapter, don't process input. They can't be powered, because they power themselves. The only value that determines how they function is their position. See Chapter 6 for more on exploiting them.

Powering Blocks

One important redstone trick that you should know about requires no extra redstone devices: All it needs is a solid block. Sometimes, if you hook up a block to your circuit, you can charge the block itself, powering all mechanisms adjacent to the block. In addition, if a block is powered with an amount of charge, the same amount of charge is given to adjacent mechanisms. The following sections show you how to apply this powerful trick.

Understanding which blocks can be powered

Because blocks can be powered only if they're complete and solid, the following blocks *cannot* be powered:

- **Blocks that are not meter cubes,** including blocks that are slightly smaller than normal ones (such as fence posts, beacons, chests, and stairs) and larger blocks such as beds, doors, and pistons. The End Portal Frame is an exception, and it can be powered.

- **Transparent blocks,** such as see-through blocks and blocks containing empty space, including glass and ice (but not *packed ice,* which is ice made opaque). The slime block is an exception, and it can be powered.

  If your graphics are set to Fast mode, leaf blocks don't appear transparent — however, they still cannot be powered.

- **Glowstone blocks:** A special case; it's a solid block, and you can even place redstone dust on it, though it cannot be powered. This feature makes glowstone an interesting material to use in circuits. However, you cannot place redstone torches, repeaters, or comparators on it.

All other blocks — dirt, wood, solid diamond — can be powered using the methods described in the following section.

Making a block powered

You can power a block in one of these ways:

- **Run redstone wire into the block.** If powered redstone wire runs into the side of a block, the block is powered. If the dust makes a trail that doesn't connect with the block, the block is not powered, even if the dust occupies an adjacent space. Interestingly, the powered block does *not* power other redstone dust, so you can assume that it's given a charge of 1.

✔ **Run redstone wire on top of the block.** When redstone dust is powered, it powers the block beneath it.

✔ **Place a redstone torch beneath the block.** As long as a redstone torch is active, it powers the block above it.

✔ **Place a redstone repeater or redstone comparator next to the block, facing it.** These machines both power blocks.

✔ **Place a button, lever, detector rail, tripwire hook, or pressure plate on the block.** These mechanisms, which are detailed in Chapter 3, always power the connected block when activated.

Applying powered blocks

Blocks are useful for transferring power neatly and efficiently. They provide an easy way for single devices to power other machines in all directions. Thus, Minecraft has a few particularly neat uses for powering blocks:

✔ **Splitting up a current through several repeaters:** Repeaters have only one output, so this tactic is useful for delivering powerful energy to many places at one time.

✔ **Improving the range of redstone torches:** This capability is useful because it allows redstone torches to disable other redstone torches (if the second torch is placed on the powered block). You can also use this feature to neatly power items such as redstone dust from underneath — it's one of the most efficient ways to carry a charge upward.

✔ **Maintaining particular levels of charge:** Many machines require the careful manipulation of charge — for example, the daylight sensor, described in Chapter 3, produces signals of varying strengths. Unfortunately, redstone dust decreases in strength the farther it travels, so using it may compromise your results. Powered blocks are useful here because they can store any charge and output the same. Thus, a combination of blocks, comparators, and redstone dust can change current however you want.

✔ **Using mechanisms to power many targets:** Connecting machinery to levers and buttons can be cumbersome — you don't want to have your input devices covered in delicate, unaesthetic redstone circuitry. Fortunately, these objects power the blocks they're attached to — for example, you can place a lever on a wall and use it to power a machine on the opposite side of the wall.

Figure 2-19 shows a few examples of powered blocks in various arrangements. Try to find other interesting uses as well.

In Survival mode, blocks are cheap resources!

Figure 2-19: All the orange blocks are normal blocks, though the functionality of each machine depends on its charge. Note that all redstone lamps are turned on.

Preventing blocks from being powered

Sometimes, powering blocks can be a nuisance. Your circuit may connect where you don't want it to, because a couple of blocks happened to become powered. Follow these suggestions to keep your blocks unpowered and ensure that your circuit runs smoothly:

✓ **Use redstone responsibly**:

- Don't put mechanisms directly under redstone dust trails.

- Don't place blocks directly above torches.

- Be sure that your redstone dust is directed so as not to power nearby blocks — unless you intend it to.

- Try to use a minimal number of blocks in complicated designs.

- Watch out for redstone dust that isn't connected to anything, which takes the appearance of a red blot — it can power all the blocks next to it.

You may encounter the arrangement shown in Figure 2-20 while trying to get a circuit working. Note that the torch powers the block above it, which activates the dust, which powers the block below it and deactivates the torch. Thus, the machine rapidly flip-flops back and forth, eventually burning out (see Chapter 4). This is usually not its intended purpose. This arrangement is a classic example of powered blocks that disrupt the function of a machine.

Figure 2-20: Setting these four objects in this way is an easy mistake to make.

✓ **Expand your machine.** Build a "blown-up" prototype of your machine, if possible. This sort of draft should separate each component of the machine and connect them with long trails of redstone dust. This strategy prevents your components from interacting with each other where you don't want them to. Do this in Creative mode (if you're working in Survival mode, create a new world for testing) so that you can easily fix your machine and make it more concise.

✔ **Use unpowerable blocks.** If you truly need to place a block somewhere for functional or aesthetic purposes but it keeps getting powered when it isn't supposed to be, try this technique as a last resort. Basically, recall that certain blocks cannot be powered. For example, glass is a useful unpowerable aesthetic block. You can also use glowstone blocks and upside-down stair blocks, which allow redstone dust to be placed on top but cannot be powered.

3

Using Redstone to Power Mechanisms

In This Chapter

▶ Activating redstone devices
▶ Powering mechanisms through redstone
▶ Building mechanisms with minecarts
▶ Designing simple machines

*C*hapter 2 introduces the various ways to transmit and manipulate redstone power. This chapter focuses on the application of these ideas. You can use many different physical machines to create power in circuits, from buttons and levers to tripwires and sensors — and many other machines can be affected by the output of these circuits. This chapter shows you what these machines are and the ways in which you can apply them.

Using Mechanisms to Activate Redstone Devices

You can use many different power-producing blocks (such as levers or buttons) to power nearby redstone devices. These mechanical blocks can be activated by players, entities, or other properties of the Minecraft world, and they can provide power in various ways.

All mechanisms described in the following list can be triggered by entities (such as a player, a chicken, or even an experience orb, depending on the mechanism) and can be placed only on other blocks. When one of these mechanisms is activated, it powers all other mechanisms adjacent to it, as well as the block it's placed on (as described in Chapter 2). Here's a rundown of these mechanisms and how they can be activated:

✔ **Lever:** You can place a lever on the top, bottom, or side of a block. When you pull the lever by using the Use Item button (right-click by default), the lever begins emitting continuous power. You can turn off the power by pulling the lever again.

✔ **Button:** You can place a button on the top, bottom, or side of a block. Like the lever, a button can also be activated by using the Use Item button. However, rather than provide continuous power, the button provides power for a short time before it deactivates and can be pushed again. Buttons can be made of either stone or wood. The only difference between the two types is that you can activate the wooden button by shooting it with an arrow, and the button provides power as long as the arrow is there.

✔ **Pressure plate:** This mechanism can be placed only on top of a block. However, though others in this list can be placed only on powerable blocks, you can also place pressure plates on fence posts. A pressure plate provides continuous power as long as an entity is on top of it. Each of the four types of pressure plates is powered differently, depending on which entities stand on it, as described in the following list:

  • *Stone pressure plate:* Activates whenever a living entity (often referred to as a *mob*) steps on it. For example, players, zombies, and chickens can activate it, but not minecarts, boats, or items.

  • *Wooden pressure plate:* Can be activated by any entity, even small ones such as items or experience orbs.

  • *Iron and gold pressure plates:* Officially called *weighted pressure plate (heavy)* and *weighted pressure plate (light),* respectively. A weighted pressure plate outputs power when any entity lands on it. However, the signal strength it produces is proportional to the number of entities on the plate at the same time. A gold pressure plate increases its strength by 1 for every entity on it, whereas an iron pressure plate does this for every ten entities. Note that a stack of items acts as a single entity. For example, to increase the signal of an iron pressure plate, you would need either ten chickens or 640 diamonds.

✓ **Tripwire hooks:** You can place tripwire hooks only on the sides of blocks. To use them, place two hooks at the same height facing directly at each other, and place pieces of string in a straight line between them. When an entity touches the tripwire, as shown in Figure 3-1, the hooks and their attached blocks become powered. If the tripwire is destroyed, the hooks become briefly powered and then turn off again. This effect doesn't happen if a player uses the shears item to disable the tripwire.

Tripwire hooks

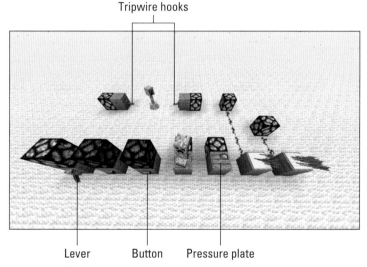

Lever　　Button　Pressure plate

Figure 3-1: When activated, these mechanisms power the block they're on as well as everything adjacent to the block.

You also have a few other ways to power redstone, with more unique properties:

✓ **Daylight sensor:** This block constantly outputs redstone power with strength equal to the amount of daylight in the sky. It can do this even while underground, and it shuts off at night. This block is useful for making devices that depend on the time of day, such as a wall around your house that rises at sundown and retracts at sunrise.

✔ **Blocks:** You can get a circuit started by simply placing normal blocks in the proper place — blocks can stop current and even become powered themselves. You can therefore power redstone by placing blocks or activating pistons. (See the next section for more on pistons.)

✔ **Containers:** As detailed in Chapter 2, you can use redstone comparators to produce charge equivalent to the storage space of a container. You can drop items into hoppers (described in the next section) or place items in chests to power redstone devices.

Powering Machines with Redstone

Whereas the previous section describes mechanisms that can power redstone devices, this section introduces some mechanisms that can be powered by redstone. When these mechanisms are powered, they perform certain actions, as described in the following list (see Figure 3-2):

✔ **Dispenser:** This block can hold as many as nine stacks of items. When powered, it launches a random item from its inventory in some direction (depending on which way the dispenser is facing). This has some interesting possibilities: The dispenser can shoot arrows and fire charges, use buckets of water and lava, apply bone meal, throw snowballs and splash potions, place and ignite TNT, hatch monster eggs, and cause fire with flint and steel. If the dispenser uses any other item, it throws away the item by a few blocks.

✔ **Dropper:** This block is similar to the dispenser except that it doesn't attempt to use the items it contains — it simply spits one out every time it's powered. In other words, if you don't want any of the dispenser's fancier functions (shooting arrows or using buckets of water, for example), just use a dropper instead. The dropper also has another useful property: If a dropper is facing and directly adjacent to another container, it places an item into the container when powered (whereas the dispenser just drops the item on top of the container).

✔ **Note block:** This block plays a musical note when powered. The instrument depends on the texture of the block directly below it — for example, wooden blocks produce a bass sound, and stony blocks produce drum sounds. You can right-click the block to change its pitch.

 ✔ **Piston:** When powered, this block extends outward into an adjacent space, pushing any blocks in its way. (Figure 3-2 shows two pistons that are extended.) A piston can push as many as 12 blocks, with a few exceptions (such as obsidian and containers). Consider also the *sticky piston* variant: When it loses power and retracts, it pulls back the block in front of the piston's extension.

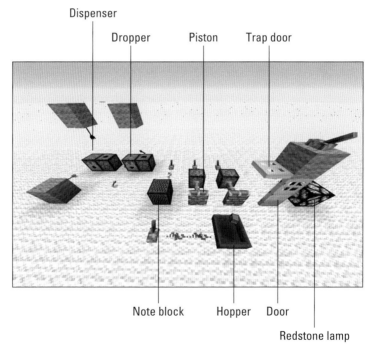

Figure 3-2: These machines can be powered by redstone.

Pistons also have some strange properties regarding how they can be powered. For example, a piston facing upward cannot be powered from above — however, when extended, its arm *can* be powered. Another strange feature is that the piston can activate when the block above it is powered, but *only* after an adjacent block is *updated* (destroyed, added, or modified).

✔ **Door and trapdoor:** Gateways such as doors, trapdoors, and fence gates open when powered and close when unpowered. Though all these items can be made of wood, and can also be opened manually by the player, doors and trapdoors have an iron variant that can be opened only with redstone power.

✔ **Redstone lamp:** Used in many examples throughout this book, the redstone lamp turns on when powered, providing light within a wide radius.

✔ **Hopper:** The hopper is an interesting automatic device, taking all items directly above it and depositing them to other containers. However, this function can be halted by powering the hopper with redstone: While powered, it doesn't receive or output any items.

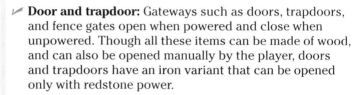

Using Minecart Mechanisms

The first part of this chapter describes blocks that produce and absorb redstone power. However, many of these blocks also have variants in the field of minecart engineering. *Minecarts* are vehicles that can carry entities and certain blocks along tracks — as such, many specialized minecarts and tracks help you turn railroads and rollercoasters into practical machines.

Minecarts

First of all, though minecarts alone can achieve plenty by rolling over certain rails, other minecarts produce interesting effects themselves:

- **Minecart with chest:** This minecart, which contains a chest that can store items, is useful for transporting resources. It works well in conjunction with the hopper item, which can siphon these items into other containers. (See the preceding section for more on the hopper.)

- **Minecart with furnace:** If a player uses the Use Item button (right-click by default) on this minecart while holding a piece of coal or charcoal, the coal item is used up to make the minecart move on its own. The minecart can push other minecarts along with it. If you right-click the minecart without fuel, the minecart changes its course to the direction in which you're facing. If a minecart with a furnace is pushed against another minecart and then reverses its direction, it pulls the other minecart with it — it can pull as many as four minecarts in a chain this way.

- **Minecart with TNT:** If a minecart carrying explosives is destroyed by fire or a blast, or if it's destroyed while moving, it explodes. It also detonates if it falls more than three blocks and doesn't land on a rail.

- **Minecart with hopper:** This type of minecart contains a hopper with five units of storage. As such, the minecart picks up any item it touches and deposits items on any hopper it runs over. (You can place minecart tracks on top of hoppers.) It also takes items one at a time from any container directly above it, even while in motion.

- **Minecart with command block:** This type of minecart contains a command block, which is explained in Chapter 7. The command block activates whenever the minecart passes over a powered *activator rail* (described in the next section).

  Though this minecart isn't available on the Creative Mode menu, you can obtain it by typing the following command (excluding the arrows) into the chat in a world where cheating is enabled:

  ```
  /give <your username> command_block_
  minecart
  ```

Minecarts can be placed only on minecart rails, and they slow down quickly when running on any other block.

Rails

Like minecarts, rails have some useful variants. Figure 3-3 shows a track made of minecart rails, containing several special rails that can power or be powered by redstone.

Powered rail   Activator rail

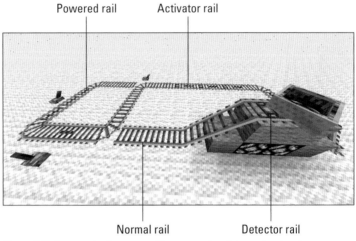

Normal rail   Detector rail

Figure 3-3: A normal minecart, rolling around an interesting track.

The four types of rails are described in this list:

 ✔ **Activator:** These rails affect minecarts when powered, and they power other adjacent activator rails. If a normal minecart passes over a powered activator rail, the minecart ejects whatever passenger it may have. Activator rails activate minecarts containing TNT or command blocks. Meanwhile, minecarts with hoppers are *deactivated*, so they don't receive or eject any items while they're on the powered activator rail.

 ✔ **Detector:** These rails have gray squares at their center. They're similar to pressure plates, providing power when a minecart — and only a minecart — passes over them. The detector rails at the top of Figure 3-3 power their adjacent booster rails when the minecart passes through, and the active detector rails just beneath the minecart are powering the redstone lamps beneath them.

✓ **Normal:** The generic minecart rail can be affected by redstone as well. If three rails converge at a single tile, the rail on that tile can bend only between two of the three paths — so it selects one of the two available elbow turns, and when powered, it switches to the other. Note the lever at the top of Figure 3-3, for example. It's next to a track that connects the right and bottom paths. When the lever is flipped, the track changes to connect the *left* and bottom paths.

 If a minecart is headed for an elbow turn that doesn't connect to its current path, it jumps the tracks slightly and continues on a straight course. The minecart shown in Figure 3-3 constantly circulates around the outer loop, although there appear to be two breaks in the track. This is useful for making minecarts go where you need them to go.

 ✓ **Powered:** Powered rails are gilded minecart rails detailed with redstone. You can see three active ones on the far left side of Figure 3-3, and see three inactive ones along the top. When active, powered rails boost the speed of any minecart passing over them. Active powered rails also activate adjacent powered rails — if many powered rails are placed in a row, all of them are charged as long as they are, at most, eight blocks from the source. If a power rail is inactive, it slows down passing minecarts, acting as a powerful brake.

Notice that Figure 3-3 uses both levers and redstone lamps in addition to the minecarts and rails; these cart systems can connect smoothly with the redstone discussed elsewhere in this book. See Chapter 5 for more about integrating more physical machines in your redstone engineering.

Connecting Mechanisms

The preceding sections in this chapter show you the mechanisms that can power redstone and be powered by redstone. This section explains how to put these components together to construct interesting creations.

Assembling simple creations

Some machines require little to no redstone dust to power them, making them cheap and easy to design. For example, in each of the three contraptions shown in Figure 3-4, the player can open the door via some mechanism (pressure plate, lever, or button), and none of them requires any complicated wiring to function.

Figure 3-4: Three simple ways to open a door. Note that the pressure plate door is automatic — you can simply walk through.

You can make simple designs like this in a few ways:

✔ **Place a powering device next to, or on top of, a mechanism.** Sometimes, simple is best. A pressure plate next to a dispenser, a lever on a redstone lamp, or a piston by a daylight sensor can all produce outstanding effects from simple concepts.

✔ **Place a lever, button, or pressure plate on a block that's adjacent to a mechanism.** You may recall that these objects power the blocks they're attached to. A wall-mounted lever can therefore power whatever is directly on the other side of the wall, and a pressure plate can similarly power items under the floor — which makes for nicely arranged machines such as the two shown on the right in Figure 3-3, or for inconspicuously hiding machines for aesthetic or devious purposes.

✔ **Use hidden levers and pressure plates to create automatic mechanisms.** An always-on lever is useful for keeping redstone lamps active. Similarly, you can use a pressure plate to activate a machine only when a certain entity passes overhead.

Connecting machines with redstone

Of course, you can do many more things with mechanisms such as levers and doors. You can activate mechanisms from afar or connect them to various programs and functions. This section shows you some basic examples for doing this; see Chapter 5 for more complex arrangements.

Long-distance connections

One of the most direct applications of redstone is connecting levers, devices, and other machines over long distances. Figure 3-5 shows a lever powering several redstone lamps in many different positions — a simple example of redstone connections. This is one of the most fundamental properties of redstone mechanics: the ability to smoothly connect input and output.

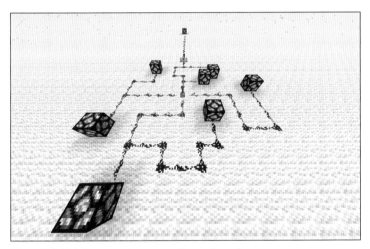

Figure 3-5: Lighting many lamps nearby, and one far away.

Simply connecting mechanisms in this way has several applications, such as

  ✔ **Activating complex machines:** Many simple and complex contraptions can be activated with a single lever or button, for example. Use trails of redstone dust to place your inputs wherever you want, such as in a door frame or a control room.

✏ **Creating traps:** A simple hidden connection can link a lever with some TNT, or a pressure plate with a piston.

✏ **Connecting several inputs to one output, or several outputs to one input:** When many items are hooked together, they can function collaboratively to produce interesting results. For example, a door might be connected to two buttons (one on either side of the doorway), or a single lever might activate a whole wall of dispensers, allowing you to rain arrows on your enemies.

Designs in multiple parts

As you can see with the more complicated designs in later chapters, creating redstone machinery is rarely a one-step process. A machine can accomplish several simple tasks to produce a grand combined result, and it often needs to take many actions to achieve its function.

As a simple example, consider a piston-powered door — a popular device that causes a set of blocks to open and close, like a door via lever. In Figure 3-6, the blue blocks form a trapdoor that opens whenever the lever is flipped. Note that the design is split into several parts and functions contributing to a single goal.

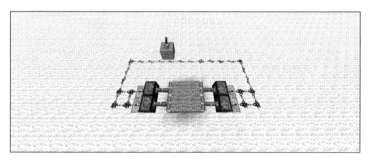

Figure 3-6: Moving four blocks via lever. All four pistons are sticky, so the device is reversible and reusable.

Figure 3-7 shows what this redstone-powered trapdoor might look like when the redstone is hidden under a gray floor.

Figure 3-7: The redstone is running underground to move the blue blocks when required.

Similarly, a number of other somewhat simple devices require a few separate pieces to assemble:

- **Player-controlled machines:** Often, a machine has levers and buttons that let the player control certain functions from afar, or complete complex functions simply. For example, a machine might allow the player to change the route of a minecart, or to craft and sort potions.

- **Choreographed events:** Many redstone devices are set up to activate various machines at programmed times. This means running a web of redstone throughout an area, often using the redstone repeater (described in Chapter 2).

- **Contraptions with complex output:** Earlier in this chapter, Figure 3-6 shows a simple example of a contraption with complex output, because four pistons must be activated at the same time. A difficult example is a machine that removes a block from a wall and replaces it with another. The first block must be pulled away, the other block must be pushed in, and none of the individual steps can interfere with each other.

Another interesting example is the always popular *TNT cannon,* which activates a group of TNT blocks and then places another TNT block shortly afterward. This causes the first group to launch the TNT at your target. Figure 3-8 shows an example, with the redstone laid out in such a way that it's easier to understand. Note that the pool of water prevents the cannon from destroying itself — TNT doesn't destroy other blocks if it explodes while submerged in water.

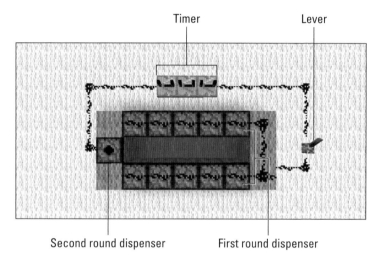

Figure 3-8: A TNT cannon is a helpful example of complex output.

Complex setups

Intricate redstone devices expand the connection of input and output, by employing large amounts of redstone and wiring to produce powerful and robust results. This might mean storing *memory* (having your circuit take particular positions to indicate settings), organizing lots of factors, manipulating lots of outputs, and more.

The most complicated designs often contain giant clusters of wiring that connect to perform functions. For example, some people like to build calculators or electronic drawing boards out of redstone. However, even these powerful contraptions boil down to simple rules and devices; see Chapter 5 for more on this topic.

4

Understanding the Laws of Redstone

Chapters 2 and 3 introduce you to the various blocks that can form redstone machines. This chapter provides an overview of the rules and techniques for putting components together. By understanding how the pieces of a machine fit together, you can better understand the process of designing redstone creations.

Exploring the Laws of Redstone

Every redstone mechanism has a different set of properties that determine how it acts. Chapters 2 and 3 examine these properties, but you should also understand the relationships between their properties. After you work with redstone for a while, the form and function of your tools can become fairly intuitive. Until then, you can use the information in the following sections to figure out what options are available to you, and how you want to assemble your devices.

The laws of power production

Figure 4-1 shows every block that can provide redstone power. The devices are surrounded by yellow and red blocks (the ones made of wool and stained glass) indicating the spaces that those devices can power: Yellow blocks indicate spaces where other devices can be powered, and red blocks indicate spaces where both devices and blocks can be powered. (You may recall that any solid block can be powered in this way, causing it to power all adjacent devices.)

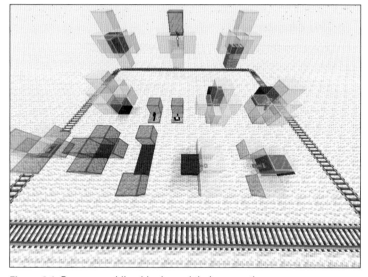

Figure 4-1: Power-providing blocks and their properties.

You can use Figure 4-1 as a guide for constructing redstone machines more intuitively, as long as you remember the following rules:

- ✔ To use one device to power another, place the device in one of the yellow or red spaces.

- ✔ To split a redstone current into several different outputs, place a solid block in a red space, and place some devices next to the block.

- ✔ Don't put a block that can be powered in a device's yellow or red space, and don't put a block in a device's red space, unless you want it to be powered by that device.

I added the yellow and red spaces in the figure for your convenience; they don't appear in your game. You should learn to visualize redstone connections and understand what links to what; this is an important skill to practice if you want to design quickly and efficiently.

The laws of power reception

Similar to what I say in the preceding section, if a device can be powered by redstone current, it has rules for how it can be powered. Figure 4-2 shows every device that can be affected by redstone power. Each block has one or more blue blocks adjacent to it (made of glass or wool) — these blue blocks indicate the direction from which the device can be powered. In other words, a device can be powered only if the power source is in the place of one of the blue blocks.

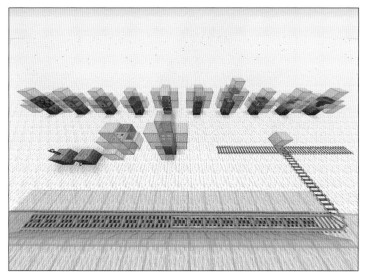

Figure 4-2: Power-absorbing blocks and their properties.

Figure 4-2 is useful for connecting redstone devices. As long as you recall how each block can be powered, you should have no trouble knowing how to integrate them into your machines.

Designing Space-Efficient Redstone Machines

A space-efficient machine in Minecraft is one that takes up very little space, occupying as few blocks as possible while still achieving its intended function. Space-efficient machines help preserve room and resources, but they're also useful for building complex machines in which many parts must interact neatly with many others.

Figure 4-3, for example, shows two devices built for the same purpose: The device on the right is a more efficient version of the one on the left.

Figure 4-3: Making a design more space-efficient.

To improve the efficiency of your designs, you can

✏ **Map out the design.** Sketch out the components, inputs, and outputs on paper or in a drawing program, and connect them with lines or arrows to indicate how your machine should function. This drawing can give you a better idea of the essential arrangements that must turn up in your machine.

✐ **Use the fundamental laws of redstone torches, redstone repeaters, and powered blocks.** Figures 4-1 and 4-2 are useful guides to see exactly how redstone fits together. Don't hesitate to split up your machine with solid blocks and build in any direction you can. If a block is powered when it shouldn't be, remember that you can place redstone dust on glowstone, on upside-down slabs, and on upside-down stairs, though none of these blocks carries a charge.

✐ **Expand on ideas from other users.** Many Minecraft players like to design interesting, compact machines and share them online. You can find them in many different places, from video sharing sites to forums, and a simple search on the Internet can produce many interesting results. These machines can be helpful in getting you started with a project — just don't try to pass them off as your own ideas in videos, forums, or other venues.

Building Some Essential Redstone Devices

To get you started with the concepts of redstone programming, I examine a couple of helpful subtopics to apply in your world, either as standalone machines or combined with other circuits. These machines can be implemented fairly easily, but they apply redstone connections in interesting ways, and they're helpful exercises for understanding redstone engineering.

 This section doesn't cover more technical devices such as logic gates and memory latches — if you're looking for those, see Chapter 5. Also, for devices based mainly on hoppers and pistons, see Chapter 6.

Producing sensors

A *sensor* is a simple example of redstone tinkering — it detects changes in the world and responds in kind, turning on a light, activating a machine, or doing whatever else is required.

Sensors can be useful in making the player's daily routine more efficient, or in neatly automating the tasks of other redstone circuits.

The daylight sensor is an example of a block that achieves this effect: It outputs different levels of power based on the time of day (zero during the night; maximum during midday), so it can tell you exactly how light it is outdoors when hooked up to an output. For example, if a daylight sensor is attached to a redstone lamp by a redstone wire 12 blocks long, it activates the lamp in the late morning and deactivates it in the early afternoon. This block is the only one that's built specifically to be a sensor, but the redstone comparator can achieve similar effects by measuring the fullness of containers.

Figure 4-4 shows a couple other examples of sensors:

✓ **On the left:** This dispenser powers the lamp above it after it runs out of items, indicating that it needs to be reloaded.

✓ **On the right:** This chain of hoppers (imagine a pipe that items automatically fall through) powers the column of lamps as items are sent down, displaying the progression of items from the top to the bottom.

Figure 4-4: Sensors hooked up to redstone lamps.

Building automatic minecart machines

Another popular device is the automatic minecart machine, a machine that involves unmanned minecarts rolling around on their own to produce various effects. Minecarts can be useful in achieving many effects that classic redstone circuits cannot do as easily. This list describes some of the unique properties of minecarts:

- **Minecart tracks carry entities, not redstone charge.** A minecart can travel along tracks when pushed by players or powered rails, but it can also fall when no block is beneath it, and be pushed in any direction when moved by a nearby piston arm. This makes the minecart a versatile way to carry information.

- **Minecarts make normally immobile blocks movable.** Minecarts can contain, chests, hoppers, furnaces, and more — this means that they can transport machines that generally cannot be moved automatically, even by pistons. Minecarts can even hold mobs such as chickens and creepers, allowing you to transport them with no trouble.

- **Minecarts follow different rules, have different physics, and run on different features.** For example, redstone repeaters can easily delay a current, whereas delaying a minecart is trickier. However, minecarts let you easily change the direction of a rail, whereas redirecting a redstone current isn't as useful. When confronted with a programming problem, it's sometimes useful to ask this question: "Is this a redstone problem or a minecart problem?"

Sometimes, redstone and minecart machines function well together. For example, a redstone loop can constantly switch a track back and forth, or a minecart can roll around several detector rails to power various redstone devices at separate intervals. See Chapter 2 for the capabilities of both redstone circuitry and minecart physics so that you can understand where either might be applicable.

Automatic minecart machines can be used for many different purposes, from transporting items and entities to activating devices along a path of any shape and size. Figure 4-5 shows an example of one such machine.

Figure 4-5: A minecart machine that runs on its own, powered by a button and some booster rails.

The device shown in Figure 4-5 is a sort of adjustable dispenser. The button on the front changes which minecart is positioned over the hopper, and the lever allows it to siphon its contents into the output chest below. If each minecart contains a different selection of items, the player can call for whichever items she wants and have them appear in the chest in front of her.

Basically, whenever the button is pressed, the chest at the bottom is sent to the top of the queue (as the booster rail beneath it is powered), and the chest at the bottom of the queue is dropped to where the first minecart was. By turning the lever to the Up position, the hopper becomes unpowered and starts absorbing items from the minecart above. (Note that rails can be placed on top of hoppers, and that items can be carried through the rails.) Building devices like these can be tricky if you don't have much practice, but as with all redstone, understanding how it works is the key step in learning the process of minecart engineering.

5

Designing Logic Gates, Loops, and Other Devices

In This Chapter

▶ Learning your NOTs, ORs, and ANDs

▶ Applying loops and recursion

▶ Stringing together interesting devices

To make more complex and intricate redstone devices, you need to know the basics of cleverly manipulating redstone current. This chapter introduces you to *logic gates,* which are powerful arrangements of redstone that can be connected and combined to produce many different machines. I also explain other creations that add interesting functions to your redstone designs.

Designing Basic Logic Gates

In redstone programming, a *binary input* of a device is any block that affects the device when powered. Every binary input can have two possible states: powered or unpowered. A *logic gate* is a function that converts one or more binary inputs into a single binary output.

Figure 5-1 shows an example. The blue blocks contain some mystery function, with binary inputs on the right (the two levers) and an output on the left (the lamp). Note that the top input is powered, the bottom input is unpowered, and the output is powered. If you flip a lever, or both levers, the output might change state, depending on the function. For example, the output might be powered as long as one lever is flipped but not the other, which makes the mystery function a useful device for locking doors or comparing blocks.

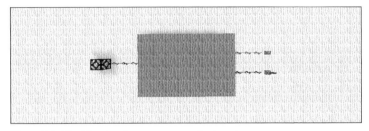

Figure 5-1: The blue box is your average logic gate.

A logic gate is essentially an arrangement that produces power depending on the variables it receives. The use of *conditional* power sources, which are activated only when certain restrictions are met, is vital in the creation of complex redstone contraptions.

To start off an exploration of logic gates and their applications, I describe the most fundamental gates: NOT, OR, AND, and XOR.

The NOT gate

The *NOT gate* outputs the opposite of its single input. For example, if the gate is powered, it outputs no power; and if the gate is unpowered, it outputs power. The NOT gate is one of the most useful gates you will use, because it outputs whatever the input is *not*. For example, if you want to make a machine that activates whenever a chest is empty or a button is released, hook up the machine to a NOT gate.

Designing a NOT gate is fairly straightforward if you read about the basic properties of redstone in Chapter 2 — most importantly, that you can turn off a redstone torch by powering the block to which it's attached. A redstone torch, therefore, *is* a NOT gate, and the attached block is the input; the torch is on while the block is off, and the torch is off while the block is on.

Figure 5-2 shows three simple designs for NOT gates, with the input levers at the top and the outputs (the redstone lamps) at the bottom. In each case, when the lever is activated, the block that's connected to the torch is powered, and the torch deactivates.

Figure 5-2: Three NOT gates with small but important differences.

The OR gate

The *OR gate* takes multiple inputs, but is simpler than the NOT gate. It outputs power if at least one of its inputs is powered — it turns off only when every single input is not powered. In other words, if an OR gate takes two inputs, it outputs power if the first input *or* the second input is powered. The OR gate requires no fancy blocks or techniques — all you have to do is connect each input to the output.

Figure 5-3 shows two simple examples of OR gates. The one on the left is a popular setup for an automatic door with pressure plates on either side of the door. Both pressure plates (inputs) activate the door (output) when powered. The example on the right, which is less aesthetic, simply shows how the connection of two levers produces a simple OR gate.

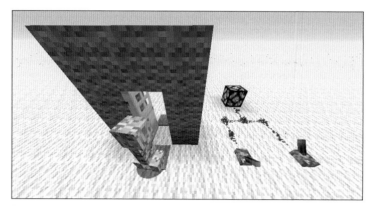

Figure 5-3: Both OR gates are active because each has one powered input.

OR gates can take more than two inputs. Just connect a bunch of inputs with a string of redstone dust.

The AND gate

Unfortunately, Minecraft has no simple block or method for creating an *AND gate*. The reason is an interesting theorem regarding binary logic: Any gate can be created with a combination of NOT and OR gates. Minecraft pretty much provides you with NOT and OR, but you have to build the other ones — such as the AND gate — from several other redstone items.

The AND gate activates only when *every* input is powered, which is harder to program than you might think. Before you let any input power the output, you must first check to see whether the other inputs agree. This list lays out the thought process behind designing an AND gate with two inputs:

1. **The AND gate must be some combination of NOT and OR gates.** This means that the AND gate must be either a NOT gate or an OR gate, with more NOT or OR gates as the inputs.

2. **Assume that one input is unpowered.** You have the NOT gate at your disposal, so what would happen if one of your inputs was *not* active? In fact, you know exactly what would happen, regardless of the other input: The AND gate wouldn't produce power, because one of the inputs is unpowered.

3. **Turn the AND into an OR.** According to Step 2, if the first input is not powered *or* the second input is unpowered, the output is not powered. Notice that this definition uses nothing but the NOT and OR functions!

4. **Determine what AND means.** Let A and B be inputs. You can rethink the definition of "A and B" to mean "not neither A nor B." In other words, the AND gate is equivalent to this combination of NOT gates and OR gates:

```
NOT ((NOT A) OR (NOT B))
```

You're done! The AND gate is simply a combination of three NOTs and an OR. Thus, to design an AND gate, you just need to follow these steps:

1. Apply a NOT gate to each input.

2. Connect the results with an OR gate.

3. Attach the whole thing to another NOT gate.

Figure 5-4 shows two examples of an AND gate: the one on the right takes only two inputs, and the one on the left takes as many as seven. The repeaters in the larger one prevent the redstone from interfering with itself, because repeaters provide power in only one direction.

Figure 5-4: Two fundamental AND gates.

The XOR gate

The XOR gate is complicated, but it's also quite useful — and a good example of combining the AND gates, NOT gates, and OR gates to interesting effects. The two-input XOR gate (short for "exclusive or") outputs power if one of the inputs is active, but *not* the other. In other words, it's powered whenever its two inputs have different values.

So how do you go about building this gate? The *exclusive or* function basically means, "Either A without B or B without A." Thus, you can rewrite XOR as

```
(A AND (NOT B)) OR (B AND (NOT A))
```

Figure 5-5 shows what a XOR gate might look like. The blue wool blocks signify AND gates and NOT gates, and the redstone lamp can be powered from either side, thus forming the OR gate.

Figure 5-5: An XOR gate, with all the wiring laid out.

Unfortunately, this design looks rather messy, especially because the output is surrounded by redstone circuitry — it will be difficult to hook this into a circuit. Figure 5-6 shows an XOR gate that is simpler and more compact, though much harder to decipher by sight.

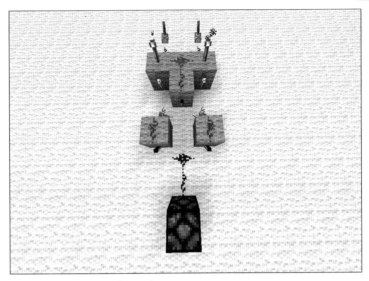

Figure 5-6: A popular XOR design.

If you look closely, you can see that this design has several similarities to the one shown earlier, in Figure 5-5. The whole design is governed by an OR gate, and each lever deactivates two redstone torches when flipped (though in Figure 5-6, both torches are on the same block). However, note how the AND gate shown in Figure 5-6 (on top of the four connected blue blocks) functions differently: It's placed in such a way that it can completely shut down the output when activated. In this way, the XOR gate performs just like an OR gate, with an extra AND to function as sort of a kill switch, ensuring that the output doesn't turn on when both inputs are activated.

This efficient XOR design employs an interesting trick for gate construction. If you put two NOT gates in a row, they cancel each other out, and the second one outputs whatever went into the first one — unless something is placed between them. You can make a kill switch by powering the space between the NOT gates, causing the second one to output as false. If you think of Figure 5-6 as two double-NOTs, with the AND gate acting as a kill switch for both, it makes the device look a lot simpler.

Devices such as this one can be tricky to design from scratch — it often helps to build creations by linking existing designs. The XOR gate is a good advanced example, but the XOR itself can be used as a component in still larger creations.

If you add a NOT gate at the end of an XOR gate, the result is a gate that tests whether its outputs have the *same* value, which is useful in devices that involve comparisons. This gate is often called the XNOR ("exclusive nor") or IFF ("if and only if") gate.

Examining Loops

A *loop* is any function that repeats itself. For example, a redstone loop might cause a piston to repeatedly activate and deactivate, a sensor to constantly check for a certain variable, or a device to iterate at regular intervals. A loop is useful for constructing devices that work consistently and constantly, without needing a player to repeatedly flip a lever or push a button.

The following sections introduce you to some of the different loops you can design and show how you can implement them.

Constructing a loop

Though a loop can encompass your entire device, the simplest loops are small machines that oscillate between two states and can be connected to the rest of your contraption. Figure 5-7 shows three basic loops that you can hook up to any input in order to make your machine flip back and forth between powered and unpowered.

Figure 5-7: Loops made of repeaters and comparators. (Redstone torches burn out if flipped back and forth too quickly.)

Loops with repeaters

The first two loops shown in Figure 5-7 rely primarily on repeaters; as I mention in Chapter 2, repeaters are blocks that pass along redstone power after an adjustable delay. In the arrangement on the left, redstone power moves slowly around the ring — this forms a loop because the machine is constantly revolving and each part of it is repeatedly being turned on and off. The arrangement in the middle is similar, but much more rapid.

To set either of these loops in motion, follow these steps:

1. **Place the blocks where you want them.**

   You get a currently unpowered loop.

2. **Place a power source to charge the loop.**

   You can place the power source anywhere, as long as it charges part of the loop. For example, for the loop on the left side of Figure 5-7, you have to power one of the blue blocks (by, say, placing a redstone torch beneath it). Note that Step 3 must come immediately after Step 2.

3. **Destroy or deactivate the power source, leaving the redstone power isolated.**

   Perform Steps 2 and 3 in quick succession (that is, place a redstone torch or block and then immediately destroy it). If you wait too long, the entire loop ends up becoming powered, and you have to destroy and replace part of the loop to reset it.

   If you don't want to have to complete this process for a simple looping device, try out the loop described in the next section (which requires more advanced materials to build, but is simpler and more efficient).

Loops with comparators

Look at the arrangement on the right side of Figure 5-7 — it's an easy-to-make loop. You may recall that a redstone comparator, if its third torch is active (which it is), subtracts from its input power the power entering its side. The arrangement shown in the figure oscillates between maximum power and low power, so a device that's a sufficient distance away will rapidly switch between powered and unpowered.

The comparator loop works as long as the front and side of the comparator are connected. You can then hook up some repeaters in the way to slow it down.

The comparator loop is one of the most useful loops available because

  ✓ **It's compact.** You can easily fit this loop into your design.

  ✓ **It's fast.** The arrangement in the figure blinks quite rapidly.

  ✓ **It's easily activated and deactivated.** Note that the loop in the figure is powered by a lever. When the lever is turned on, the loop immediately starts cycling; when the lever is turned off, the loop shuts down. This means that a comparator loop, unlike the loops in the previous section, is easy to start and stop.

Other loops

You can build loops in a number of other ways. For example, you can connect two hoppers (see Chapter 6) or set a command block (see Chapter 7) to destroy and replace an adjacent redstone torch or block.

Here are a few general principles to remember when designing your own redstone loops:

  ✓ **The loop must have at least two different states, each of which invokes another.** Almost every block-updating process takes a moment to work — loops must exploit this delay. Your arrangement should update in such a way that it always returns to its original state, thus cycling infinitely through different states.

  ✓ **The loop must always contain a catalyst.** In other words, something must keep the loop in motion. As long as the loop is active, it should not include a state that has no reason to update or change.

  ✓ **Timing is everything.** If a loop isn't timed well, it may lock up and cease to function. Suppose that the loop shown in the middle of Figure 5-7 has one repeater at maximum delay and the other repeater at minimum delay. In this arrangement, redstone current moves faster on one side of the loop than on the other, and the powered segment ends up catching up with itself, powering the entire loop and stopping its motion. To avoid this situation, make sure that the delays in your loop are distributed evenly, and test your design to look for places where the current might be moving too fast.

A long chain of redstone repeaters is a useful method for designing a very slow loop. It also can help you visualize the structure of a loop, because you can easily see the string of redstone current racing through the repeaters.

Implementing loops

It's surprisingly easy to make a machine run repeatedly — all you have to do is connect it to the output of a loop. For example, in Figure 5-8 a dispenser loaded with fire charges is connected to a comparator loop, causing it to activate rapidly.

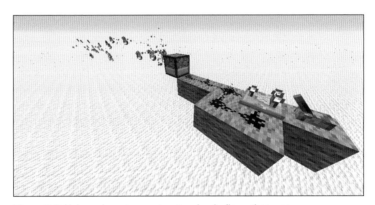

Figure 5-8: Using a loop to construct a simple flamethrower.

Of course, in Minecraft you have more ways to integrate loops into your designs. Figure 5-9 shows an advanced example: a loop made of redstone repeaters that automatically constructs and repairs a huge cobblestone wall. Exploiting the concept that water and lava mix to create cobblestone, as well as the piston's 12-block limit, the loop is connected to two sets of pistons, alternating between them to push the freshly made blocks sideways and upward.

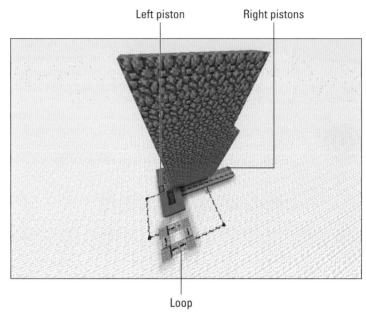

Left piston   Right pistons

Loop

Figure 5-9: Building a wall with a single loop.

The implementation of loops in these devices is an example of *recursive* programming: applying the same function multiple times for practical purposes. This is a widely applicable field in Minecraft — if you ever want a program to run continuously or repeatedly, simply use a loop.

Manipulating Redstone Strength

Recall that redstone carries not only power but also a certain level of power — the *strength* of the current. In previous versions of Minecraft, this was simply a limit on how far redstone dust can be stretched before the current has to be refreshed. However, the strength of redstone can now be manipulated and applied to produce more elaborate machines.

Figure 5-10 shows a simple example of this technique. The comparator can pass different levels of charge to the trail of redstone dust, which in turn activates a different number of redstone lamps, depending on its strength. The machine is reading the storage space of the chest on the left and telling the player that it's now two-thirds full (10 of the 15 lamps are activated).

Figure 5-10: Partially powering a redstone circuit.

This concept is quite useful because you can conditionally activate output in your machines. You can manipulate and apply redstone strength in a few different ways:

- **Use low-strength current.** A circuit with very low strength can save a lot of space and apply all the benefits of limited-strength redstone. For example, you can connect two redstone torches to the back and side of a comparator, with one slightly farther away than the other, to produce a strength of 1. You can also use a container connected to a comparator so that the strength switches between 0 and 1 or between 1 and 2.

- **Connect a row of mechanisms to a row of redstone dust.** If a string of redstone dust can take many different possible charge strengths, it can power many different possible mechanisms as well. For example, you can set a row of redstone repeaters next to the dust or set some lamps or command blocks below it.

- **Compare redstone strengths with comparators.** Comparators can test one redstone signal against another, and even take the difference of the two signals.

Constructing Various Useful Redstone Devices

You can construct many other simple but essential redstone devices in Minecraft. The process behind building them is similar to the gates and loops explained earlier in this chapter, but the purpose of these devices is more specific and often more practical. The following sections introduce you to some of them and describe how they work.

Implementing memory

When designing a redstone machine, it's quite helpful to have that machine remember important information. For example, your computer remembers all of its settings and downloads, and some functions need to keep track of its inputs while working them out. This is where *memory,* the ability of machines to store data, enters the picture.

Figure 5-11 shows two *memory latches,* which are devices that store information. Both latches have the same arrangement of blocks, but they're powered in different ways. The memory latch is similar to the loops described in the "Implementing loops" section (earlier in this chapter) because the same device can take multiple positions; however, rather than cycle back and forth on its own, the memory latch must be triggered manually. Note that the left side of the latch becomes powered if the left button is pressed, and that the right side of the latch is powered if the right button is pressed.

Figure 5-11: A memory latch and its two settings.

A memory latch functions like a lever because it can flip between two positions. What makes it unique, however, is that each position is associated with a different input. The button for turning off the memory latch is different from the one for turning it on. In this way, you can have one button work as an activator and another button work as a reset switch — in the meantime, the memory latch stores whatever bit of data is sent to it.

This concept is extremely useful, for a number of reasons. You can

- **Design a machine that stays activated even when its power source is deactivated.** Current often flows constantly through a redstone machine — memory latches are wells of information that retain their structure unless directly modified by a reset switch.

  For example, Figure 5-12 shows four compact memory latches (marked with diamond blocks) connected to comparators. Even when the comparators no longer provide power, the memory latches remember that they were activated in the past. The memory latches can be deactivated only by a reset switch, connected to the line of redstone repeaters in the background.

- **Tile memory latches together to produce RAM.** Though the memory latch in Figure 5-11 isn't space-efficient, you can use repeaters to make latches that can be tiled together compactly. Then you can hold a lot of data for complex devices such as minigames — and use these arrays to detect, update, and reset information.

- **Attach static devices to dynamic contraptions.** In the earlier section "Examining Loops," I explain how hooking a loop to a machine can make the whole thing oscillate between two positions. If you wire a memory latch to a machine, however, you can use it to maintain a stagnant piece of information that isn't affected by the machine's inner workings.

  For example, you can connect a memory latch to a contraption that activates only during a certain condition. In this way, the latch is powered not when the machine is currently powered, but rather when it had been powered sometime after the latch was reset. Essentially, the memory latch remembers the state of a circuit instead of acting on it instantly.

If you ever want to connect an input and an output but you don't want the output to start right away — and you need it to wait for some other condition — a memory latch is extremely useful.

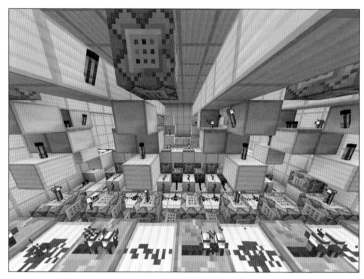

Figure 5-12: Memory latches wired into a circuit.

Designing a block update detector

Another useful machine is the *block update detector,* which is often referred to as a *BUD switch.* This machine provides a pulse of redstone power whenever it detects that an adjacent block has been updated — that is, when the block's status or properties have been modified in any way. The BUD detects these types of changes: blocks being destroyed and placed, furnaces being loaded, or jukeboxes being played, for example. The BUD functions somewhat like a loop, but with a small glitch: It iterates only when reminded to do so.

Figure 5-13 shows a popular BUD design, which can be extended and reshaped in many different ways (especially with slime blocks, as explained in Chapter 6).

You can implement BUDs in your machines in many different ways:

✏ **Detect natural block changes.** For example, you can have a machine that activates whenever a nearby tree grows or fire spreads to a piston.

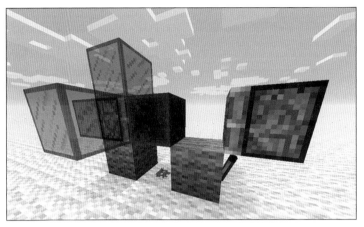

Figure 5-13: A BUD switch. The red stained glass doesn't contribute to the switch — I used it to indicate the spaces where updates can be detected.

✔ **Activate machines by placing or destroying blocks.** This is a good way to power redstone devices without using levers, buttons, and the like.

✔ **Turn beds, jukeboxes, and other updatable blocks into input machines.** Activate other machines by sleeping in beds, placing records in jukeboxes, or cooking items in furnaces, for example.

Most simple BUDs are made with pistons because of their unique way of processing redstone current. The BUD shown in Figure 5-13 uses two normal pistons, though single sticky pistons can work as well. Essentially, the block update must make the piston notice that it's being powered and correct itself, only to revert quickly. The technique behind designing a BUD seems to be "Make a machine briefly contemplate a logical fallacy."

Building redstone vertically

Another useful trick for designing effective redstone circuits is laying out circuits vertically rather than horizontally along the ground. Building devices at different angles can allow them to fit together better and function well within different areas, such as in a crawlspace or between other machines. For example, Figure 5-14 shows the AND gate (see the earlier section "Designing Basic Logic Gates") remade flat against a wall.

Figure 5-14: A sideways redstone gate, powered by two levers.

Building redstone vertically requires a bit more intuition, but these tips can help:

- **Remember the rules for powering blocks.** In particular, recall that you can place redstone torches under a block or redstone repeaters next to it, and every device next to the block becomes powered. This is useful for efficiently transferring vertical redstone current.

- **Use the full extent of your redstone library.** Trails of redstone dust don't do much for you here — vertical wires can run only straight, upward, or downward. Use lots of torches, repeaters, and the like to make the circuit run properly and efficiently. In addition, torches and repeaters can be placed directly next to each other without interfering, so it makes the circuit easier to copy and tile together.

- **Diagram the purpose of your device.** Compact vertical devices can be tricky to understand because many of the components end up powering multiple blocks at a time. If you draw out the machine you want to produce (circuit diagrams can be particularly useful in this regard), building these machines can become much easier, and it's definitely easier to understand other people's designs.

6

Using Physical Machines in Redstone Devices

● ●

In This Chapter

▶ Using pistons, containers, and other items to manipulate items and blocks

▶ Sorting, farming, and gathering resources automatically

▶ Mastering the use of powerful mechanisms such as hoppers and slime blocks

● ●

*T*hough redstone programming generally refers to the transfer of intangible energy from input to output, a number of features allow you to transfer other information, including items and even blocks. These physical machines combine with redstone electricity to create item sorters, flying machines, entity managers, automatic farms, tricks and traps, moving platforms, and much more.

This chapter shows you the functions and applications of some physical redstone devices. You may have seen some of these in previous chapters, but they have a number of hidden uses when combined with other entity-moving mechanisms.

Moving and Sorting Items between Containers

Items can be difficult to manage. Collecting, sorting, and arranging them is often a challenge to players who want their resources available and efficient. This section shows you some redstone tricks, particularly those concerning the hopper block, for manipulating collections of items and even implementing them into other devices.

Implementing and connecting hoppers

A *hopper*, described in detail in Chapter 6, is a funnel-shaped block that automatically receives items into its five-slot storage and moves them to another container. The top of the funnel is open, and the bottom can point down or to any side, depending on whether the hopper is placed on the top or side of a block.

The hopper's functions are described in this list:

- ✔ **Collect any item in the space directly above the hopper.** Just like other containers, hoppers have inventories which can store items, and any item directly above a hopper is automatically sent to this inventory. This means that you can throw items into the funnel to fill the hopper, but it also means a lot more. If a hopper is placed underneath a container — such as a chest, a dispenser, or another hopper — the hopper gradually absorbs items from it (taking five items every 2 seconds). However, if all five of the hopper's inventory slots are full, it does not absorb items. For example, if all five slots are filled with swords, it doesn't accept any more items. If all five slots contain sand, it takes only sand (until a full stack of sand is in each slot).

- ✔ **Dispense items from the bottom of the funnel.** Just as hoppers automatically take items from above, they give these items to whichever container they're hooked up to. If the end of the funnel isn't connected to anything, the hopper retains the items, and they must be manually removed by a player.

- ✔ **Cease all function when powered by redstone.** If a hopper is powered, it doesn't receive or dispense items. You can't even throw items into the funnel. After the power is cut, the hopper resumes as normal.

What makes a hopper a fundamental component in this aspect of redstone is that a hopper transfers items from one place (the top) to another (the bottom or side). Figure 6-1 shows a few hopper-based designs that transfer items to chests.

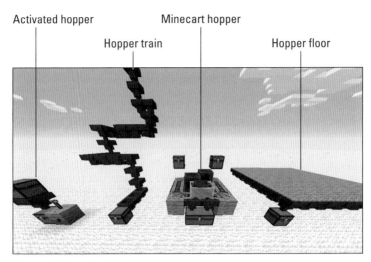

Figure 6-1: Arrangements of hoppers for various purposes.

The concepts, from left to right, are described in this list:

✒ **Activated hopper:** This hopper sends a few items from the top chest to the bottom chest when the button is pushed. Such a device could be used like a vendor, or a new sort of dispenser.

✒ **Hopper train:** All these hoppers are connected, so if an item is placed in any one of them, it eventually works its way to the chest at the bottom. You can, therefore, automatically channel items between different areas.

✒ **Minecart hopper:** This hopper rolls around, collecting items from above and distributing them below, allowing you to easily distribute or gather items from many different containers. Note that minecart rails *can* be placed on top of hoppers, and that the activator rails prevent the minecart from dispensing items in certain places.

✒ **Hopper floor:** These hoppers, obscured from the top by carpets, absorb any item that lands on the ground and siphons that item into the chest in the corner. If you want to collect any item that falls on the floor, especially loot from enemies or recovered equipment from players, this is the most direct way to do it.

You cannot place multiple chests next to each other — two chests make a double chest, which works fine, but a third chest cannot be placed in this way. However, if you alternate between using chests and trapped chests, you can bypass this restriction — trapped chests are just chests which can activate nearby comparators when opened, but they can be placed next to normal chests.

Using hoppers to distribute items

Though a hopper technically has only one input and one output, its features can be useful for dividing up items. Figure 6-2 shows an interesting arrangement of three hoppers: The hopper in the upper-left corner has its items being collected by *both* of the other hoppers.

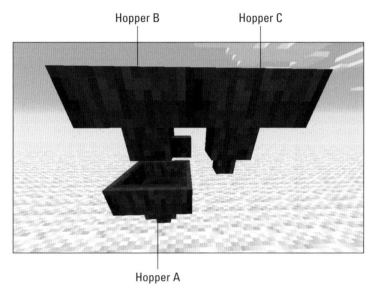

Figure 6-2: Hopper A is taking from Hopper B, which is giving to Hopper C. Thus, Hopper B loses items on two fronts.

Items in this arrangement are distributed fairly evenly from Hopper B to Hoppers A and C. This strategy is an interesting one for filling multiple containers at one time: Both are filled at the same time, and when one becomes full, all items are diverted to the other (because a full hopper doesn't receive any more items).

However, you can apply this distribution trick in another useful way: sorting. You may recall that a hopper cannot accept items if they don't fit in its inventory. A hopper full of stackable items, therefore, can accept only more of that item. Thus, if the hopper shown at the bottom of Figure 6-2 has, say, a fish in each inventory slot, it picks out only the fish from the items in the hopper above (while the third hopper gets the rest of the items). Because a 0.4-second delay always occurs before an item is either sent or received, the hopper below generally takes priority over the one to the side — a hopper can take an item from below faster than it can receive and then give an item. Thus, if you want to sort items by using this method, the hopper at the bottom of Figure 6-2 should be the sorter.

Figure 6-3 shows another version of this technique. Every hopper behind an item frame is loaded with the item shown in that frame — the item frames aren't necessary for the machine to work, but they remind the player what is being sorted and where. After players spend the night fighting mobs, they can place the subsequent rewards in the chest in the upper-left corner, and the hopper will filter the items (bones and iron, for example) into the corresponding chests. Note the use of the comparators: These items ensure that the sorting hoppers have a certain number of items in them before they start filling the chests. (Otherwise, they give out the items that they're using to sort.)

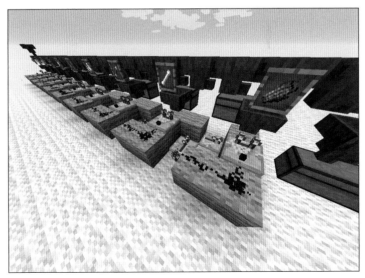

Figure 6-3: This sorting machine can be generalized to sort out any number of item types.

Building item-based circuits

You can design a number of interesting circuits to move items around and gain some advantage as a result. A few of these are explained in the following sections.

Automatic furnaces

A furnace is an essential part of any game in Survival mode: By placing an item in one slot of the furnace and fuel in the other, you can cook them into different items. When an item is sent automatically to a furnace, it goes to one of these two slots — items sent in through the top are placed in the top spot, and items sent in through the side or the bottom are placed in the bottom slot. This makes the *automatic furnace* — a furnace that cooks several stacks of items without being manually loaded by the player — quite a popular concept.

Figure 6-4 shows an example of an automatic furnace. It's a simple design that constantly pumps items into the furnace until it's full or the chests run out of items. The item frames in the figure represent the item filling the chests behind them — coal is sent through the side to be burned, and raw beef is sent through the top to be cooked into steak.

Figure 6-4: A basic automatic furnace.

Storage cellars

As you progress through Minecraft and obtain lots of items or build large automatic farms to obtain huge amounts of certain items, you need a place to put them. Unfortunately, large rooms full of treasure chests can be tedious to manage, and the effectiveness of an automatic farm is limited by the size of the container it fills. To solve this problem, you can use hoppers to implement a sort of storage cellar.

Figure 6-5 shows two examples of storage cellars. In the simple storage cellar on the left, the items in the chests are constantly being siphoned downward by the hoppers. The lowest chest fills up first, and then the hopper above it, and then the chest above that, and so on. Thus, the stack of chests functions as a single unit that fills from the bottom, bearing many times the storage space of a single chest. The other storage cellar design on the right is more compact, but just a bit more resource-intensive.

Figure 6-5: Two storage cellars built aboveground.

Item-powered circuitry

Just as items can be moved and sorted with circuits, items can be used to modify circuits. Because items can come in many different quantities and be transferred by hoppers like physical wires, they can make interesting contributions to your contraptions, including these possibilities:

- **Compact, precise timers:** Fill a container with items and connect it to a hopper and comparator. As the hopper removes the items, the charge through the comparator slowly decreases. This causes the container to act as a sort of timer, with its time proportional to the number of items placed in it.

- **Randomizers:** Dispensers and droppers eject random items from their inventories when powered. As noted in Chapter 2, items with a small stack size produce a greater charge in a redstone comparator. Thus, a dropper containing eight stackable items and a sword could place one of these items into a dropper-comparator setup, producing a charge of 2 with a 1-in-9 chance.

- **Locks and keys:** The earlier section "Using hoppers to distribute items" outlines how hoppers can be used to sort items. You can, in fact, use hoppers as door locks. A stack of hoppers, including a sorter, can require players to insert a certain item in order to pass through the door.

Pushing Blocks Around with Piston Machines

The preceding section explains how to move items around in circuits — here, we examine the manipulation of blocks. This extremely useful concept lets you build everything from giant doors to moving platforms to killer robots.

The following sections provide some tips for using blocks such as pistons and slime blocks to revise the structure of your world's creations.

Hooking pistons together

 A piston has a fairly simple function: When powered, it extends an arm 1 block in a certain direction, pushing up to 12 blocks along with it. The sticky piston is a commonly used variant that can also pull a single block when the arm retracts. When combined and applied creatively, these blocks can be extremely powerful tools.

One important aspect of using pistons is that they can be tiled easily, so you can assemble a long row or an entire sheet of pistons to move many blocks at a time. Pistons have strange rules for how they can be powered (see Chapter 2 for the full explanation), but they support interesting arrangements such as the ones shown in Figure 6-6.

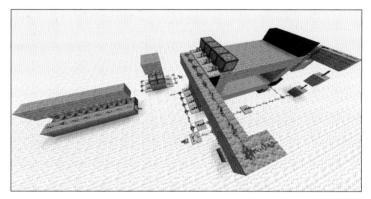

Figure 6-6: Using pistons to raise walls, create platforms, and run simple conveyor belts.

The two arrangements shown on the left side of Figure 6-6 are fairly simple ones — when a lever is thrown, a wall or platform is raised or retracted. The large arrangement on the right is sort of a crude conveyor belt: The rectangular strip of blue blocks is constantly being cycled around in a loop, as sets of pistons take turns pushing it around.

Pistons can even be used to push entities, from items and minecarts to mobs and players. For example, you could hide a piston behind a wall on a ledge to push unsuspecting zombies over the edge. As long as you remember that pistons can push multiple blocks at a time, you can use them to make your world more dynamic in all sorts of ways.

Pushing powerful blocks

Of course, pistons don't have to be used solely for output — you can actually use them as integral components in your circuits. For example, if redstone runs up the side of a block, you can break the connection by pushing a block in its path. However, there are a couple blocks (as described in the following sections) that are particularly useful when pushed around by pistons.

Moving redstone blocks

The redstone block is the only device that can power adjacent mechanisms *and* be pushed by a piston without breaking. This makes it an incredibly dynamic concept, because it can be moved about to provide power to different parts of a circuit. Also note that, because of how pistons are powered, a piston can hold a redstone block directly in front of its arm without being powered by it.

Figure 6-7 shows a couple of applications of this concept. The one on the left is a simple machine that alternates between powering the redstone dust and the redstone repeater, showing the ability of a simple movable redstone block. Though the one on the right is less practical, it shows how redstone blocks can create chain reactions to produce completely physical machines (applying only tangible blocks).

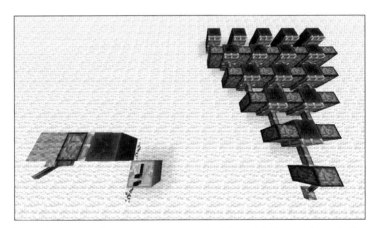

Figure 6-7: Translating power sources with pistons. All pistons shown in the figure are sticky pistons.

Thus, if you want your redstone circuit to be a bit more dynamic, use pistons to move around the power source.

For a simple application of this theory, simply place a redstone block in front of a sticky piston. This strategy lets you move a single power source between two different positions with a simple input, such as a lever or a pressure plate. However, it doesn't work if the redstone block is *above* the piston — because of how pistons are powered, the piston cannot retract after pushing the redstone block upward.

Moving other pistons

When a piston's arm isn't extended, it can itself be pushed by another piston. This greatly improves the capability of piston machines, allowing them to combine in modular patterns.

For example, Figure 6-8 shows a design for pushing something twice the length that a normal piston can. Much like pushing redstone blocks (see the earlier section "Moving redstone blocks"), this concept can make circuits much more dynamic and structurally interesting.

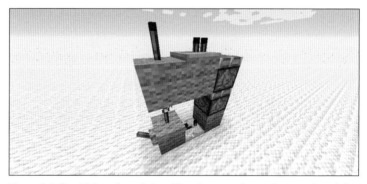

Figure 6-8: Combining piston joints. The piston on the top is normal, and the piston on the bottom is sticky.

Essentially, the repeater at the top can power the top piston only after the bottom one has pushed it upward. Thus, the two repeaters next to the pistons are timed such that

- ✏ **Whenever the lever is activated,** the bottom piston pushes the top piston into the powered top repeater, causing the top piston to extend as well.

- ✏ **When the lever is deactivated,** the top piston retracts first, and then the bottom piston pulls it backward.

As long as you make sure that a piston is retracted before you move it with another piston, you can chain together pistons in any orientation and any arrangement.

You can design a chain of sticky pistons that extends several blocks forward and then retracts to its original position. However, if you do this, you must make the pistons retract in the reverse order in which they were extended. This is because a piston cannot push or pull an already extended piston, so each piston must retract before the one behind it.

Sticking blocks together with slime blocks

Another extremely useful block in piston devices is the *slime block*. Though its name may not exactly scream "mechanical engineering," the slime block has some interesting properties. Essentially, when a slime block is pushed or pulled, it moves all adjacent blocks with it. Note that slime blocks can pull *other* slime blocks, allowing you to move whole chains of them along with all the attached blocks. If you stick on some redstone blocks, slime can act as three-dimensional wiring — thus, you can build some interesting machines out of nothing but pistons, slime blocks, and redstone blocks.

Figure 6-9 shows one of these applications: a flying machine. It's essentially a vehicle that carries a group of blocks through the air, floating across the world until it bumps into something.

Figure 6-9: Pushing slime block arrangements with pistons.

The flying machine shown in the figure is composed of five separate chains, each containing a piston and a redstone block connected by slime blocks. The chains are constantly pushing each other forward — one piston is activated by a redstone block in the next chain, so it pushes the next chain forward (deactivating itself by moving the redstone block away) and causes the next chain's piston to be powered by the redstone block in the chain after that. This concept can be confusing at first, so look closely at how flying machines work in order to build your own. Figure 6-9 can help, but you can always look for more designs online.

Also note that a piston's 12-block limit still applies to slime blocks. (It can only push an arrangement of blocks if it totals to, at most, the weight of 12 blocks.) This can make the process difficult if you want slime blocks to connect two distant objects, but you can extend a slime chain's reach with the same sort of redstone-piston arrangements shown earlier, in Figure 6-9.

Use more than two pistons when building a flying machine or another loop with slime blocks. Three pistons are enough, but sometimes it's easier to use more, especially when building large machines. Pistons take time to extend and retract, so a two-piston flying machine would quickly stop in its tracks because a piston will soon try to push a retracting piston.

When building a machine that contains slime blocks, don't place the slime blocks on the ground. Your machine won't be able to run if it's trying to pull the entire world along with it!

Managing Entities with Redstone Circuits

Sometimes you want a contraption to involve entities. For example, you may want to throw an item into a machine that drops it on a random tile in a chance game, or you may want to channel the zombies from a dungeon into your neighbor's house. Though accomplishing this task sometimes requires no redstone-based items, it often follows the same principles and can be improved with a bit of circuitry.

The following sections explain how you can use either engi-neering or physics to implement these entities into various mechanisms.

Moving entities around

You can transfer entities around the world in a few ways, to get them where you need them to be:

✔ **Piston:** As explained in the previous section, a piston can be used to push objects around in all directions, including entities — you can push them up, down, or to the side. This item is useful for moving entities that are constrained to small areas, such as raising a creeper on a small platform or pushing some items over a thin ledge.

✔ **Water:** A channel of flowing water is good at pushing entities in a certain direction. For example, if you build a farm to automatically produce items, you can build a stream that funnels all dropped items into a hopper. Note that mobs always attempt to swim up to the surface of water, so a vertical waterfall makes a good elevator for leading creatures upward (though even undead can hold their breath for only a limited time).

✔ **Ice:** Entities such as items can be thrown or dispensed onto a trail of ice, where they slide for quite a long dis-tance before stopping. Blocks of packed ice achieve the same effect, except that they can also be powered by redstone current.

✔ **Bait:** You can also make entities move by calling on their behaviors. For example, a villager in a well-defended minecart can lure zombies; a snow golem can aggravate nearby mobs with its snowball attack; wheat can attract pigs and cows; and cats can scare away creepers. It's an effective way to guide mobs to — or away from — certain areas and contraptions.

You can use any of these methods to move entities wherever you want in your circuit.

Using entities as input in redstone circuits

In this section, you can find out exactly what the point is of moving entities around with engineering. Whether it's throwing items around or guiding mobs toward certain areas, entities and their behaviors can be surprisingly useful in programming.

Here are just a few ideas for what you can do with these concepts:

✔ **Mob-powered randomizers:** Set pigs, slimes, or other mobs in a room containing one or more pressure plates. Because the mobs move around fairly randomly, they can trigger a circuit at random intervals.

✔ **Item input:** Use dispensers, hoppers, and ice to move items around your circuit. This way, players can throw items into the machine to make it run, or item-harvesting farms can transfer its produce to a specific container or onto a pressure plate.

✔ **Mob farms:** You can build special "farms" that turn Minecraft's constant waves of mobs into a constant supply of items — this involves manipulating both mobs and items. See Chapter 11 for more information on these arrangements.

An empty minecart can contain a mob. Mobs enter minecarts automatically, and activator rails can eject them. In addition, mobs avoid crossing over minecart rails. Thus, entity-based circuits also work well with minecart tracks.

Building Circuits and Machines with Minecart Tracks

Minecarts and rails are Minecraft features often used for transporting players. However, they can also perform a lot of mechanical feats better than the usual redstone items.

Minecarts are entities that can roll quickly along minecart rails. They can turn, go up and down slants, and even derail (though they suffer a large amount of friction off the rails, slowing to a halt almost immediately). Minecart rails generally have these properties:

- **Each rail can be straight or bent at a right angle.** When a rail is placed or updated, it automatically connects to any open-ended rails directly adjacent to it, if possible. If a rail is adjacent to three open ends such that it can make two possible elbow turns, it bends in a direction dependent on whether it's redstone-powered. Booster rails, detector rails, and activator rails cannot bend in elbow turns, and can only face straight between two opposite directions.

- **Straight rails can automatically connect to rails one block above or one block below.** Rails can run at an upward or downward angle — you just have to arrange some blocks in a staircase pattern and place the rails on top of them. This concept is similar to the redstone dust property of running up the sides of blocks, but slightly more limited — if a minecart rail is in the form of an elbow turn, you cannot connect it to other rails in this way.

- **If a minecart "jumps" onto an elbow turn, it continues to move in a straight line.** Some minecart tracks involve running a minecart rail into an elbow turn — but not from one of the open ends. If two tracks are adjacent without being connected, and one is facing the other, the minecart automatically jumps from one track to the other and continues moving in the same direction as when it jumped.

Though redstone is run by an intangible current, minecart machines are run by placing one or more minecarts on a track and setting it going, often in an infinite loop (assisted by booster rails). In this way, working with minecarts is a more object-oriented science, focusing on components and their properties rather than on functions.

You can fill minecarts with chests, furnaces, hoppers, TNT, and command blocks. See Chapter 3 for more on the different types of minecarts and rails, and how you can apply them.

You can also push minecart rails with pistons. (You push the rail itself, not the block it rests on.) This makes pistons useful in minecart-based circuits. Pistons can move rails from one track to another, push several rails at a time to extend them outward, and even completely rearrange tracks to change the route of some minecarts. However, you should keep these points in mind when using pistons with minecarts:

- **You cannot push minecart rails up or down.** If the block under a rail is moved vertically, even if the rail is moved at the same time, there will be a moment when the rail and the block are separate, and thus the rail will break. You can move the block under a rail horizontally, but only if you move the rail itself in the same direction simultaneously.

- **Minecart rails automatically connect to other rails when pushed or pulled.** When a rail is moved so that it's next to the open end of another rail, it automatically changes its direction and can even change between a straight track and an elbow turn.

- **Minecarts can be pushed along with rails.** If a minecart is on a rail, a piston next to the rail can push both of them at one time, and the minecart should stay on the rail. This doesn't work when pulling a rail with a sticky piston, because it cannot pull entities such as minecarts.

Though minecarts are more physically limited than redstone, they have advantages that make their mechanics worth learning. For example, you can send a minecart through a long track that activates machines in different positions at different times. You can also move objects such as hoppers and command blocks around in tracks and loops, producing effects that are difficult to obtain with classic redstone. Thus, if you want a program to be simple but dynamic, build it with minecarts.

Understanding Other Applications of Physical Machines

Earlier in this chapter, I describe many different types of physical machines, from item management to piston contraptions to entity manipulation. These ideas are quite versatile, so you can apply them in plenty of ways. This section examines some more interesting ideas that you can try out for yourself.

Building an automatic farm

You can build farms in Minecraft in many ways — you can farm wheat from stalks, mushrooms in darkrooms, and iron ingots from iron golems, for example. In fact, many of these farms can be completely automated. The earlier section "Managing Entities with Redstone Circuits" covers part, but not all, of this topic. For example, you can harvest wheat by pushing fully grown stalks into a hopper via piston, or you can farm chickens by collecting their eggs in a hopper and hatching them with a dispenser.

Figure 6-10 shows an interesting example of an automatic farm: a cactus farm. A cactus block cannot be placed directly adjacent to another block — thus, whenever a cactus in the figure grows, the top part is broken by the adjacent block and becomes an item. These items then fall into the water below, which is directed at the hopper at the center, filling all the chests stacked at the bottom.

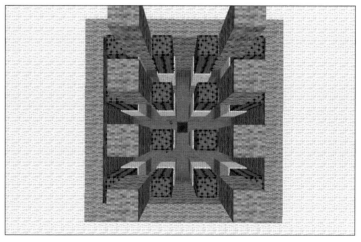

Figure 6-10: An automatic cactus farm. You can make it bigger by turning the base into a funnel shape to make the water flow farther.

You can build other farms by pushing entities off ridges with pistons, connecting plants to block update detectors (or BUDs, as explained in Chapter 5), applying bone meal (a plant growth catalyst) with dispensers, for example. Get creative!

Programming fancy doors and locks

You can combine pistons in many different ways to move around various groups of blocks. This concept is often used in the popular field of designing fancy doors: doors made of several blocks that can be pulled apart and pushed together with a simple input, such as a lever or a button.

Figure 6-11 shows a simple example of such a door (doorframe not included) — it's built to be flat enough that it can fit inside a building. The lever can be placed anywhere as long as it connects with the redstone dust at the bottom.

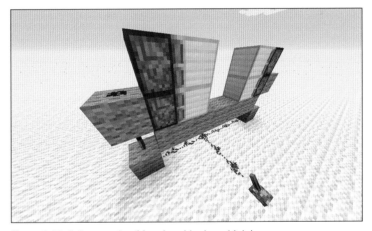

Figure 6-11: A door made of four iron blocks, which is open.

Bouncing entities with slime blocks

Slime blocks have the odd property of being sticky and bouncy at the same time — and, in fact, both properties have applications in the field of redstone. Slime blocks can bounce any entities that land on them, especially when pushed against the item with a piston. For example, Figure 6-12 shows a series of piston-powered slime blocks that are bouncing items toward the left.

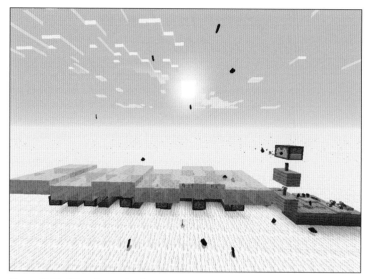

Figure 6-12: Slime-bouncing fun.

You can do this with players, mobs, items, or active TNT, for example. They let you build interesting transportation devices, cannons with powerful range, and various other machines for getting entities from one place to another quickly.

7

Introducing the Command Block

reative mode in Minecraft contains a redstone-based block so important that it requires several chapters to fully explain. This block — the *command block* — dramatically improves the scope of what you can do in the game and allows you to manipulate the world automatically on a large scale. You can program the command block with a text interface and activate it by way of redstone power. Because of its usefulness in designing creative worlds and custom challenges (as described in Chapter 10), this versatile block is essential to master for the complete redstone experience. This chapter shows you how to use a command block and how to program every command it supports.

Throughout this chapter, I sometimes provide you with incomplete commands, where you have to fill out certain data yourself, such as usernames and coordinates. (Don't worry: I'll show you how to do this.) I use two sorts of brackets to mark this data, which is standard in Minecraft-speak: arrow brackets (<...>) indicate required arguments, and square brackets ([...]) indicate optional arguments. For example, if a command includes the "<player name>" parameter, I might type "Isometrus" instead.

Obtaining a Command Block

 Command blocks, because of their world-bending abilities, cannot be found in Survival mode. In fact, they don't even appear on the Block menu in Creative mode. To obtain a command block, you must follow these steps:

1. **Create a world that enables cheats.**

   If you start your world in Creative mode, cheats are enabled by default. You can tell whether cheats are enabled by finding your world on the Select World page — the third row of text should contain the word *Cheats.*

 2. **Clear out a space in the inventory.**

   Preferably, at least one of the nine bottom inventory slots should be clear.

3. **Open the chat menu.**

   You do this by pressing the T key by default.

4. **Type** `/give <your username> command_block.`

   If you opened the Chat menu with the Open Command key (which is / by default) rather than the T key, the slash at the beginning is entered automatically.

5. **Press Enter.**

   The command block should appear in the inventory. If the bottom row of the inventory was already full, open the full inventory (press E by default) to find the command block.

   Congratulations — you now have your first command block!

Programming and Activating a Command Block

You can place the command block like you can place any normal block. By right-clicking on the block (or using a non-default Use Item button), you open the Set Console Command for Block interface, as shown in Figure 7-1. You can enter a command in the Console Command box, which is the black box shown at the top of the figure. You can access this interface only in Creative mode — if you're playing on a server, you must have operator status as well.

Reminders   Console Command box

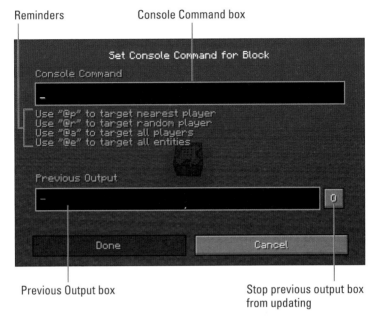

Previous Output box   Stop previous output box
                                       from updating

Figure 7-1: The Console Command box contains the command you set. The Previous Output box tells you what happened when the block was powered last.

Minecraft has many commands that you can enter in the chat interface, which can do various things, from teleporting the player to manipulating blocks. By entering one of these commands into a command block rather than the chat interface, you can execute the command automatically and remotely by powering the block.

A *command block* is a solid, nontransparent block, so when it's powered a certain way, it activates everything around it. (See the section on powering blocks in Chapter 2.) This can be useful for powering multiple command blocks easily, but it can also mess up the work of inexperienced designers.

The simplest way to use a command block is to place a button, lever, or pressure plate on or near the block — this allows you to activate the command block whenever you want. Some players like to take many command blocks and hook them up to redstone circuits, a process detailed in Chapter 9. For now, I examine the form and function of a single command block.

Applying Different Commands

Commands are functions that can be executed in any world that enables cheats, as described in the earlier section "Obtaining a Command Block." Many commands are easy to apply, and others are intricate and complex. All commands are multiple strings of text separated by spaces. Each string starts with a word identifying which command you're using, followed by a few *parameters,* which are numbers or strings that specify how the command is executed.

Suppose that a command named `togglecakefall` makes cake rain from the sky. (At the time of this writing, no such command exists.) This command requires two parameters: how long the rain lasts and what type of cake is produced. An execution of this command might look like this:

```
togglecakefall 800000 fruitcake
```

The translation: Fruitcake falls from the sky for 800,000 ticks (40,000 seconds).

In the commands discussed in this chapter, you see arrow brackets such as `<parameter>` and square brackets such as `[parameter]`. When you fill out these parameters, do *not* include the brackets. Arrow brackets represent required parameters. Square brackets indicate optional parameters, which have default settings and thus don't matter if you leave them out. However, if you leave out one parameter, you may not include any parameters beyond it, or else the computer will get confused. For example, take the command `clear <player> [item] [data] [maxCount] [dataTag]` — if you want to use the maxCount parameter, you have to include the item and data parameters too, even though they're normally optional. In addition, some parameters are split up by vertical bars, like `<clear|rain|thunder>`. This indicates that the parameter only has a few possible settings (in this case, "clear," "rain," and "thunder").

You can use any of the commands by typing them into the chat interface — however, if you do this, you must type a slash (/) in front of the command. Also, each chat message has a maximum length, so you have to use the command block to execute long commands.

The following sections tell you all about the basic commands, which can be used with only a few *parameters* (extra inputs), and advanced commands, which require many, often complex, parameters.

Basic commands

Basic commands can be applied easily, requiring only a few words and numbers. Command blocks support the following basic commands.

```
defaultgamemode <mode>
```

Specifies the game mode for new players entering the world. For <mode>, you can enter survival, creative, adventure, or spectator or the numbers 0, 1, 2, or 3, respectively.

Getting help on the Chat menu

If you forget a command, you can enter /help (or /?) on the Chat menu to see the first page in a list of commands. Here are some additional ways to get help in the chat interface:

✔ To view other help pages, type /help <page number>. Replace <page number> with the page number you want to see.

✔ To view the parameters needed for a specific command, type /help <command name>.

Replace <command name> with the command for which you need help. (Don't use a slash with the command name.)

Note that some parameters in this chapter are listed as mandatory, whereas the Minecraft Help files list them as optional — this is because some commands can be executed by command blocks only if certain parameters are specified.

```
difficulty <new difficulty>
```

Sets the difficulty level of the game. For `<new difficulty>`, you can enter `peaceful`, `easy`, `normal`, or `hard` or the numbers `0`, `1`, `2`, or `3`, respectively. This strategy works even if the world's difficulty is *locked* (preventing players without cheats from changing it), so keep this command block away from the wrong hands.

```
gamemode <mode> <player>
```

Changes the game mode of the target player. For `<mode>`, you can enter `survival`, `creative`, `adventure`, or `spectator` or the numbers `0`, `1`, `2`, or `3`, respectively.

```
kill <target>
```

Instantly kills whoever the target is. You can enter a username for `<target>` to kill a specific player's avatar or use the special arguments described in the later section "Implementing Special Arguments in Commands."

```
me  <action>
```

Displays a third-person statement in the chat. If I enter `/me is building a house`, the chat would say `* Isometrus is building a house`. The command block's name is `@` by default, making this command produce weird messages, such as `* @ says hi`; however, you can use the anvil block to rename the command block, allowing it to produce messages such as `* The Great Command Block says hi`.

```
say <message>
```

Just like the `me` command, except that it's formatted more like a normal chat message. When activated, it prints `[<command block name>] <message>`.

```
seed
```

The number from which the world is derived — in other words, two worlds with the same seed are created the same way. When this command is run from a command block, the seed of the world is outputted in the Previous Output box of the command block interface.

```
tell <player> <private message . . .>
```

Produces a message in chat that only certain players can see. The target receives the message `<command block name>` `whispers to you: <private message . . .>`. You can also use `msg` or `w` as alternatives to `tell`.

```
tellraw <player> <raw json message>
```

Lets you send more-intricate text messages to the target player(s). However, the message must be in JavaScript Object Notation (JSON) format, which can be complicated to use. Fortunately, websites such as `http://ezekielelin.com/tellraw` allow you to produce these messages with a buttons-and-menus interface.

Figure 7-2 shows how a `tellraw` command can be used to produce intricate and interactive messages.

Figure 7-2: The player hovers the cursor over the green 5 to display the popup text.

```
time <set|add> <value>
```

The time of day, represented by a number between 0 and 24000. This number constantly increases, but when it reaches 24000, it cycles back to 0 again because a full day and night have passed. This means that the daytime begins at 0 and nighttime begins at 12000. This command lets you manipulate this number. The first parameter can be `set` or `add`, which determines whether you're setting the time to a certain value or adding a number to its current position. `<value>` is the number in question.

```
title <player> <title|subtitle> <raw json
title>
```

Displays a large string of text in the middle of the target player's screen. The text fades in, lingers for a while, and then fades out again. If the second parameter is `title`, the text is immediately displayed in this way. If the second parameter is `subtitle`, text is displayed as a subtitle under subsequent titles. The text itself is the final parameter, and it can be either simple text or in JSON format.

```
title <player> times <fadeIn> <stay>
<fadeOut>
```

A different application of the earlier `title` command; defines for the target player some individual settings that modify how titles are displayed. The last three parameters are all numbers representing how long the title should take to appear, how long it should stay, and how long it should take to disappear. The numbers are measured in *ticks,* or 20ths of a second.

```
title <player> <clear|reset>
```

Another application of the earlier `title` command. If the second parameter is `clear`, the title displayed to the target player is removed instantly. If the second parameter is `reset`, all of the player's title settings (including subtitles) are returned to their defaults.

```
toggledownfall
```

Alters the weather. If it's raining, the rain stops — otherwise, it begins raining.

```
weather <clear|rain|thunder> [duration in
seconds]
```

Changes the weather. You can produce clear weather, rain, or a storm by setting the first parameter to `clear`, `rain`, or `thunder`, respectively. You can also include a number at the end of the command to specify the duration of the weather in seconds.

```
xp <amount> <player>
```

Gives experience points to the target player; <amount> is the number of points given. However, you can also write a capital *L* at the end of this number to grant levels instead of points. For example, xp 100L Isometrus gives the player 100 extra experience levels.

Advanced commands

These commands are trickier, but often more useful to learn. These commands require several parameters, and often work with autocompletion and coordinates.

    achievement give <stat_name> <player>

Grants an achievement to the target player. For <stat_name>, you have to enter the specific string that corresponds with an achievement. To do this without consulting the Internet, use the autocompletion feature described in the later section "Autocompleting Commands on the Chat Menu," by typing achievement, and then a period, and then pressing Tab.

Understanding X-Y-Z coordinates

Minecraft uses the variables x, y, and z to annotate positions within the world. You can press F3 to open a menu that includes your character's x-, y-, and z-coordinates. For computers with an Fn key, you'll have to press Fn-F3.

The x-coordinate increases as you go east (and decreases as you go west), whereas the z-coordinate increases as you go south (and decreases as you go north). The y-coordinate increases toward the sky, and the lowest point where you can place blocks is at $y=0$. The positions $x=0$ and $z=0$ have no real significance.

Some commands require you to enter a certain position as a parameter, with the format <x> <y> <z>. The F3 menu gives you lots of information about your position and direction, which is useful in filling out these parameters — if you want the coordinates of a certain position, move your character there to figure it out. For example, the block you're standing on always has your same coordinates, with the y-coordinate reduced by 1.

If you want to determine which way you're facing without consulting the F3 menu, remember that the sun always rises in the east and sets in the west. The moon follows the same pattern (in Minecraft, at least).

```
blockdata <x> <y> <z> <dataTag>
```

Adds data tags to the block at the target coordinates, changing its properties. See Chapter 8 for information about data tags.

```
clear <player> [item] [data] [maxCount]
[dataTag]
```

Clears certain items from the target player's inventory. If [item] is omitted, the player's entire inventory is cleared. [data] is a small, nonnegative integer that allows you to remove only a certain variant of the item. [maxCount] is the number of items to remove. (If undefined, every instance of the item is removed from the player's inventory.) [dataTag] allows you to remove only items with certain data tags — see Chapter 8 for more on this topic.

```
clone <x1> <y1> <z1> <x2> <y2> <z2> <x> <y>
<z> [mode]
```

Copies a certain box-shaped area to another location, duplicating all blocks inside the area. This is useful for building lots of houses and pillars, for example, with minimal effort. The area to clone is defined by two opposite corners, defined by the coordinates (x1, y1, z1) and (x2, y2, z2). This area is cloned to the position with coordinates (x, y, z). Because [mode] is set to replace by default, the cloning process rewrites any existing blocks. However, you can also set it to masked — with this setting, if the cloned area contains empty spaces, the empty spaces don't replace other blocks when cloned.

```
effect <player> <effect> [seconds] [amplifier]
[hideParticles]
```

Gives a special effect to the target entity. <effect> is the numerical ID of the effect — consult Table 7-1 to see which IDs correspond to which effects. [seconds] is the duration of the effect in seconds (the default is 30). [amplifier] is the strength of the effect (0 is normal strength, and higher numbers are stronger). [hideParticles] can be set to true or false (the default is false) — if true, the entity doesn't emit swirly particles indicating the effect. However, players can always see their active effects by opening the inventory.

You can also use `effect <player> clear` to remove all effects from the target.

Table 7-1		Effects
ID	*Effect*	*Description*
1	Speed	Movement speed increases.
2	Slowness	The player runs slower.
3	Haste	The entity mines blocks faster.
4	Mining Fatigue	The entity mines blocks slower.
5	Strength	Attack damage increases.
6	Instant Health	Regains health. (This effect has no duration.)
7	Instant Damage	Receives damage. (This effect has no duration.)
8	Jump Boost	The jumping height increases.
9	Nausea	The player's screen swirls.
10	Regeneration	Health is restored over time.
11	Resistance	Receives less damage. (Invincibility when amplifier is at least 4.)
12	Fire Resistance	Provides immunity to fire and lava.
13	Water Breathing	Provides immunity to drowning.
14	Invisibility	Provides an invisible body. Has various giveaways (physical contact, wielding an item, wearing armor, or on fire, for example).
15	Blindness	Sees only nearby objects.
16	Night Vision	Can see in the dark. Disastrous when combined with blindness.
17	Hunger	Becomes hungry faster.
18	Weakness	Attack damage reduced.
19	Poison	Loses health over time. Entities cannot lose their last bit of health to poison.
20	Wither	Loses health over time.
21	Health Boost	Maximum health increases. Gain two extra hearts for every effect level.

(continued)

Table 7-1 *(continued)*

ID	Effect	Description
22	Absorption	Provides extra health. When damaged, absorption health is consumed and cannot be restored.
23	Saturation	Abates hunger. (This effect has no duration.)

```
enchant <player> <enchantment ID> [level]
```

Enchants whichever item the player is holding, if the item is allowed to have that enchantment. Similar to the `effect` command, `<enchantment ID>` is a number corresponding to the enchantment, and `[level]` is the enchantment's amplifier (starting at 1).

```
entitydata <entity> <dataTag>
```

Adds data tags to the target entity, changing its properties. See Chapter 8 for information about data tags.

```
execute <entity> <x> <y> <z> <command>
```

Executes another command relative to the target entity. Using the information in the later section "Examining relative positions," you can have a command affect positions relative to certain entities. For example, the command `execute Isometrus ~ ~10 ~ summon Pig` summons a pig 10 blocks above the player Isometrus.

```
execute <entity> <x> <y> <z> detect <x2> <y2>
<z2> <block> <data> <command>
```

This command is an extension of the `execute` command. It's just like `execute`, except that the command is activated only if the block at `<x2> <y2> <z2>` has the same name as `<block>` and the data value of `<data>`. For example, the command `execute Isometrus ~ ~10 ~ detect ~ ~-11 ~ gold_block 0 summon Pig` summons a pig only if the player is standing on top of a gold block.

If you use relative coordinates for `<x2> <y2> <z2>` (see the later section "Examining relative positions"), they will be calculated relative to the `<x> <y> <z>` coordinates.

```
fill <x1> <y1> <z1> <x2> <y2> <z2> <TileName>
[dataValue] [oldBlockHandling] [dataTag]
```

Fills up an entire rectangular area with a certain block. The two pairs of coordinates (x1, y1, z1 and x2, y2, z2) in this useful command represent opposite corners of the box. `<TileName>` is the official name of the block, which can be found with autocompletion. (See the later section "Autocompleting Commands on the Chat Menu.")`[dataValue]` is a non-negative number representing the variant of the block (0 by default). `[oldBlockHandling]` decides how the filling process is handled, and it can take the following values:

- `replace`: This is the default setting. All blocks that are in the way are replaced by the new ones. However, if you add `replace` as a parameter, you can also add another `[tileName]` parameter, as well as another `[dataValue]` one, if you want — this makes it so that only a certain type of block is replaced. For example, if you enter `replace iron_block` at the end of the command rather than fill the region with a new block, the command replaces all iron blocks in the region with the new block.

- `destroy`: If a block is replaced during the filling process, it produces destruction particles, updates its position, and drops an item as though it were mined by the player.

- `keep`: The Fill command places blocks only in empty spaces.

- `hollow`: The edges of the region are filled, and the inside is replaced by air, producing a hollow box made from the block you chose.

- `outline`: The edges of the region are filled, but no existing blocks are harmed — thus, you produce a box that encloses everything inside.

Lastly, `[dataTag]` sets data tags for the block, as described in Chapter 8. Note that you cannot fill more than 4096 blocks with a single fill command.

```
gamerule <rule name> [value]
```

Block-changes a rule of the world. [value] can be true or false, setting whether the given rule applies. If you don't include [value], the command block prints the current state of the game rule in question, in the Previous Output box. Table 7-2 describes the values you can use for <rule name>.

Table 7-2	Game Rules	
Rule Name	**Default**	**Description**
commandBlockOutput	true	Each command block displays a message in chat every time it's activated. Set this to false if you use so many command blocks that your chat fills up with useless information.
doDaylightCycle	true	The day and night pass automatically. Set this to false to stop the sun and moon from moving.
doFireTick	true	Fire spreads, destroys blocks, and eventually burns out (unless it's on top of a netherrack block).
doMobLoot	true	Entities such as pigs and zombies can drop items (including equipment) when defeated.
doMobSpawning	true	Entities can appear in the world without being actively created by the player.
doTileDrops	true	Items can appear from destroyed blocks (for example, dirt from dirt blocks or string from cobwebs).
keepInventory	false	Players don't drop the items in their inventories when their characters die.
logAdminCommands	true	Keep a log of every command executed directly by the administrators of a server and every message displayed through command blocks.

Rule Name	Default	Description
mobGriefing	true	Entities can destroy and modify blocks. For example, endermen can move blocks around, and creepers can leave craters where they explode.
naturalRegeneration	true	Players' health regenerates as long as they aren't hungry. If this is set to false, players cannot recover from damage unless they use health potions, regeneration potions, or other healing items such as golden apples.
randomTickSpeed	3	At the time of this writing, this is the only game rule whose value is a nonnegative number rather than true or false. The higher the value, the more likely you are to see random natural block updates, such as the growth of plants such as wheat and trees. A setting of 0 completely prevents this from happening.
showDeathMessages	true	Players' deaths — as well as their causes — appear in chat.

```
give <player> <item> [amount] [data] [dataTag]
```

Gives items to players — it places the item in the player's inventory if possible, and otherwise drops it on the ground in front of the player. `<item>` is the name of the item — you can find it with autocompletion (see the later section "Autocompleting Commands on the Chat Menu"). `<amount>` is the number of items you give the player, and `[data]` is a nonnegative integer that determines the variant of item the player receives (for example, the color of wood planks or the remaining durability of a tool). `[dataTag]` allows you to modify the tags contained in the item — see Chapter 8 for more information.

When commands are autocompleted, the names of blocks and items all begin with `minecraft:`. However, that part of the name is unnecessary, so if you remember the name of an item, you can type it again quickly.

```
particle <name> <x> <y> <z> <xd> <yd> <zd>
<speed> [count] [player|entity]
```

Summons a bunch of particles in an area for interesting effects. `<name>` can be found with autocompletion (see the later section "Autocompleting Commands on the Chat Menu"), which is interesting to experiment with. The first set of coordinates determines where the effect is centered, and the second set of coordinates determine the width of the effect in each dimension. `<speed>` is the speed of the particles (for stationary particles, such as explosions, `<speed>` sometimes modifies their size instead). `[count]` is the number of particles you summon (the default is 1, but you often want a large number). You can even center the coordinates on a player or entity with `[player|entity]`— see the later section "Examining relative positions."

```
playsound <sound> <player> [x] [y] [z]
[volume] [pitch] [minimumVolume]
```

Similar to `particle`, it can play any sound effect for players. `<sound>` cannot be found with autocompletion, so to get the sound you want, follow these steps:

1. **Press Esc.**

    The Game menu appears.

2. **Click Options and then Resource Packs.**

    The Select Resource Packs screen appears.

3. **Click the Open Resource Pack Folder button.**

    A second window appears, showing the files in this folder:

    ```
    User/AppData/Roaming/.minecraft/
    resourcepacks
    ```

4. **Navigate to** `.minecraft/resources`.

    Go to the `.minecraft` folder and find the folder labeled `resources`.

5. **Open** newsound, sound, **or** sound3.

   All these folders contain sound files. You can also
   add your own sound files, if you want, if you have an
   original recording that you want to add to the game.
   However, if you're on a multiplayer server, only people
   who can access the file can hear the sound.

6. **Find the sound you want.**

   The value of <sound> is the data path for the sound
   file. For example, if you look inside the mob folder, and
   then the creeper folder, and find the death sound,
   you can use mob.creeper.death as the parameter.
   However, if a sound file has a number at the end, do
   not include the number, or else no sound is played. For
   example, if you play the sound step.cloth, the command randomly selects either step.cloth1, step.
   cloth2, step.cloth3, or step.cloth4.

The <player> parameter is who you want to play the sound
to. You can enter coordinates to play the sound at a certain
position (or relative to the target players), [volume] to control how easily it can be heard (1 is the default), [pitch] to
control the sound's length and pitch (1 is the default), and
[minimumVolume] to ensure that it can always be heard with
a certain volume. The last three arguments can all be decimals,
and can all be less than 1, if you want a low volume or pitch.

```
replaceitem <block|entity> <selector> <slot>
<item> [amount] [data] [dataTag]
```

This command adds an item to a particular inventory slot,
replacing the one that's already there. To modify a container
(like a chest or a hopper), set the first parameter to block,
and set the second parameter to the block's coordinates
(such as 128 60 343). If you want to modify the inventory
of an entity instead, set the first parameter to entity and
the second parameter to the entity you want to select. The
<slot> parameter says which slot you want to modify — you
can set it to any of the following:

✔ slot.armor.head, slot.armor.chest, slot.armor.
   legs, slot.armor.feet: For an entity that can equip
   armor, these are the slots for its helmet, chestplate, leggings, and boots. You can change the color of a zombie's
   suit or upgrade the items being displayed on an armor
   stand.

✔ `slot.weapon`: The item being carried by a mob or an armor stand.

✔ `slot.enderchest.#`: An ender chest displays a different inventory for each player who uses it — with this parameter, you can modify a slot of the target player's ender chest inventory. Rather than type the pound sign (#), you type a number between 0 and 26 to choose the slot — slots are numbered in increasing order from left to right, top to bottom.

✔ `slot.hotbar.#`: Modify a slot in the bottom row of the target player's inventory. Rather than type the pound sign (#), type a number between 0 and 8 to select a slot (0 on the left, 8 on the right).

✔ `slot.inventory.#`: Modify a slot in the top three rows of the target player's inventory. Rather than type the pound sign (#), type a number between 0 and 26 to choose the slot — slots are numbered in increasing order from left to right, top to bottom.

✔ `slot.horse.saddle`: The inventory slot where a horse equips its saddle.

✔ `slot.horse.armor`: The inventory slot where a horse equips its armor.

✔ `slot.horse.chest.#`: If a donkey or a mule is carrying a chest on its back, this parameter modifies a slot in that chest. Rather than type the pound sign (#), type a number between 2 and 16 to choose the slot — slots are numbered in increasing order from left to right, top to bottom.

✔ `slot.villager.#`: A slot in a villager's inventory. This does not affect the villager's trading mechanics. Rather than type the pound sign (#), type a number between 0 and 7 to select a slot (0 on the left, 8 on the right).

Finally, the last four parameters determine the item to place in the slot, the quantity of the item, the data value of the item (used for determining variants), and any data tags you want on the item. (See Chapter 8 for more on data tags.)

`scoreboard`

A versatile function with many properties and functions. To use it, see the section "Managing a Scoreboard," later in this chapter.

```
setblock <x> <y> <z> <TileName> [dataValue]
[oldBlockHandling] [dataTag]
```

Causes the block at the target x-, y-, and z- coordinates to become a new block defined by `<TileName>`. This replaces any other block that was at that position. This function works similarly to the earlier one, except with blocks instead of items: `<TileName>` can be found with the autocomplete feature, and `<dataValue>` is a nonnegative integer that determines which variant of the block you're using. Also, if there's already a non-air block at the target coordinates, it can be handled in three different ways, depending on the values of `[oldBlockHandling]`: `replace` (the default) replaces the block, `destroy` breaks the block (as though you were mining it) and then replaces it, and `keep` leaves the old block intact. `[dataTag]` lets you set the tags for the new block (see Chapter 8).

```
setworldspawn <x> <y> <z>
```

Because every world has a particular region where new players appear, changes the center of this region to the x-, y-, and z-coordinates provided. If no coordinates are entered (that is, if you simply type `setworldspawn`), the region is instead centered around the command block itself.

```
spawnpoint <player> <x> <y> <z>
```

Whenever the target player dies, he reappears at the x-, y-, and z-coordinates provided. If no coordinates are entered, the player reappears near the command block.

```
spreadplayers <x> <z> <spreadDistance>
<maxRange> <respectTeams> <player ...>
```

Used to manage groups of players by spreading them out around a center. The `<x>` and `<z>` parameters are the coordinates of the center. (You cannot change the center's altitude.) `<spreadDistance>` is the minimum distance between players, whereas `<maxRange>` is the greatest distance the players can be spread away from the center (so that they can't be pushed too far away by the command). `<respectTeams>` can be set to `true` or `false` — if `true`, then players on the same team (see the entry for the scoreboard command) are grouped together. Lastly, enter a list of the target players' usernames separated by spaces, or use a generalized argument. (See the later section "Implementing Special Arguments in Commands.")

```
stats <block|entity> <selector2> set <stat>
<selector> <objective>
```

When a block or entity executes a command (whether directly or through the execute command described above), it records information about how the command went. This command allows you to print one of those statistics onto an objective in the scoreboard (see the later section "Managing a Scoreboard").

If you're looking at the statistics of a block, set the first parameter to `block` and the second to the block's coordinates. For entities, set the first parameter to `entity` and the second to the entity you want to target. The `<stat>` parameter can take the following values:

- ✔ `AffectedBlocks`, `AffectedEntities`, `AffectedItems`: The number of blocks, entities, or items (respectively) that the last command affected.
- ✔ `QueryResult`: The output of a "query" command: this command asks a question, like `testfor`.
- ✔ `SuccessCount`: A counter that indicates whether the command was successful.

Lastly, `<selector>` refers to the entity whose score you want to change, and `<objective>` is the name of the scoreboard objective to be changed (see the later section "Managing a Scoreboard" for more on scoreboards and objectives).

```
stats <block|entity> <selector2> clear <stat>
```

This command functions much like the preceding command, except that it erases certain statistics from the target block or entity. See the preceding command to understand how the parameters work for this command.

```
summon <EntityName> <x> <y> <z>
```

Summons an entity (animal, monster, or minecart, for example) at the specified coordinates. You can also add data tags at the end of the command to customize the entity, as described in Chapter 8. `<EntityName>` is the name of the entity you want to create, which can be determined with autocomplete. (See the later section "Autocompleting Commands on the Chat Menu.") Though the classic pigs and zombies are the most apparent uses of this command, you can summon a few particularly interesting items:

- `MinecartCommandBlock`: This command block acts as an entity. It can run along minecart rails, and with the right data tags, execute some versatile commands from various locations. See Chapter 9 for more information about putting together command blocks in this way (as well as using data tags to decide what the summoned command block does).

  Minecarts don't have to be placed on rails—the rails simply help them move better. If you need to move a minecart around and don't want to use rails, you can always apply the `tp` command to teleport it.

- `Item`: This one summons an item that players can pick up. Use data tags to decide which item it is and what properties it has.

- `Fireball`, `SmallFireball`, and `WitherSkull`: If you use data tags to set this entity in motion (it disappears otherwise), you can have a lot of destructive fun with this summon command.

- `ThrownPotion` and `FireworksRocketEntity`: Again, you need data tags for this, but summoning splash potions and special effects has a variety of applications, from building custom challenges (see Chapter 10) to entertaining yourself.

- `FallingSand`: Normally, this command produces a block of sand — however, you can use data tags to make it become any block you want, which falls until it hits the ground and then becomes solid.

- `MinecartSpawner`: This entity can travel along minecart rails and summon mobs. Its data tags make it even more versatile than the `summon` command, such as summoning several mobs at one time and stopping when a certain number of entities are nearby.

```
testfor <player> [dataTag]
```

To use this command, the command block should be directly behind a redstone comparator (see Chapter 2). The command attempts to locate `<player>` and sends the comparator a signal strength equal to the number of entities found. It continues to output this redstone current until its command is changed or until the command block is powered again. `[dataTag]` allows you to look for players and other entities with certain data tags (see Chapter 8).

```
testforblock <x> <y> <z> <TileName>
[dataValue] [dataTag]
```

Similar to the earlier `testfor` command, this command powers comparators next to the command block if a certain condition is satisfied. In this case, it checks the block at the coordinates provided and gives a signal strength of 1 if the block matches the name provided in the `<TileName>` parameter. If you entered a data value or data tags, it compares those too. You can find `<TileName>` with autocompletion, as described in the later section "Autocompleting Commands on the Chat Menu."

```
testforblocks <x1> <y1> <z1> <x2> <y2> <z2>
<x> <y> <z> [mode]
```

Like `testforblock`, except that this one compares two *regions* and checks whether the arrangement of blocks is identical. The first region is represented by two opposite corners defined by (x1, y1, z1) and (x2, y2, z2), and the second region is positioned at (x, y, z). If you use `masked` for the `[mode]` parameter, the empty spaces in the first region are ignored.

```
tp <target player> <destination player>
```

Teleports the target player to the destination player.

```
tp <player> <x> <y> <z> [<y-rot> <x-rot>]
```

A more advanced version than the basic teleport command. The target player is teleported to the target coordinates. You can even set which way the player is facing with the `<y-rot>` and `<x-rot>` parameters — these are optional, but if you include one you must include the other. `<y-rot>`

is the player's rotation around the y-axis — at both 0 and
360, the player is facing south and rotates clockwise as the
number increases. `<x-rot>` is the player's rotation around
the x-axis — at both 0 and 360, the player is looking directly
ahead and rotates clockwise as the number increases. These
two parameters may be assigned relative values. (See the later
section "Examining relative positions.")

```
worldborder <add|set> <sizeInBlocks>
[timeInSeconds]
```

Creates a square blue field that damages players outside it.
It extends infinitely both upward and downward, and can
limit players to a certain region of the world. Players cannot
place or destroy blocks outside the border. The first parameter should equal `set` if you want to set the diameter of
the border, and `add` if you want to add a certain amount
to the diameter (or subtract, if the amount is negative).
`<sizeInBlocks>` is the number of blocks that make up
the length and width of the border. If `[timeInSeconds]` is
provided, the border gradually changes over that amount of
time, instead of resizing instantly. (It turns red when shrinking and turns green when growing.) You should use the
`worldborder center` command first (see the next bullet),
or else the border will be centered on x = 0, z = 0, which is
rarely what you want.

```
worldborder center <x> <z>
```

Moves the world border to the target coordinates. If you haven't
created a world border, it's centered here when you create it.

```
worldborder damage buffer <sizeInBlocks>
```

Changes the buffer margin around the world border (default-
ing to five blocks). Players outside the world border start
taking damage only if they're more than `<sizeInBlocks>`
blocks' distance away from the border.

```
worldborder damage amount <damagePerBlock>
```

Changes the amount of damage players take when they're
sufficiently far from the world border. The damage is equal to
`<damagePerBlock>` times the distance from the player to
the border. The default is 0.2 (where 1 is half of a heart on the
Health bar).

```
worldborder warning <time|distance> <value>
```

As the player approaches a world border, the edges of the screen grow an increasingly prominent red aura as a warning. This command lets you set the properties of that effect. If for the first parameter you put `time`, the aura starts to appear when the border is shrinking and is `<value>` seconds away from passing the player. If you put `distance`, the aura instead starts to appear when the player is `<value>` blocks in distance away from the border.

Autocompleting Commands on the Chat Menu

The Chat menu has a useful feature for writing commands without consulting various guides. The Tab key allows you to automatically complete commands and parameters with a single button. This makes it efficient and extremely useful to write complicated commands in chat, and then copy and paste them into command blocks with Ctrl-A (select all), Ctrl-C (copy), and Ctrl-V (paste).

If you start to type a command or parameter and then press Tab, you can see a list of every possible option, and the first one is automatically added to your command. If this isn't the one you wanted, you can keep pressing Tab to cycle through the options until you have the right one. For example, if you open the Chat menu, enter a slash (/) and press Tab, you can see a list of all available commands. Similarly, if you type `/te` and press Tab, you can select a command from `/testfor`, `/tellraw`, `/tell`, `/testforblock`, and `/testforblocks`.

Autocompleting doesn't work if there's anything to the right of the cursor. You can autocomplete only what is currently the last word of the command.

The same statement applies to parameters with a finite number of options. These parameters include

- ✓ **Blocks and items:** If a command requires a certain block or item as a parameter, you can find it with auto-completion. All block and item names are of the form `minecraft:<name>`. Press Tab to autocomplete the `minecraft:` part, and then autocomplete the rest as you would normally.

- ✔ **Achievements and statistics:** Like blocks and items, achievements are of the form `achievement:<name>` and statistics are of the form `stat:<name>`.

- ✔ **Booleans:** Parameters that can be either true or false are easy to autocomplete.

- ✔ **Player names:** If a command requests the name of a player, you can use autocomplete to select one from the list of all players in the world.

- ✔ **Command-specific parameters:** Some parameters can take only specific values, such as `replace` or `masked`. You can use autocomplete to see all available options for parameters like this.

When autocompleting a parameter, be sure to enter a space after the previous word in the command; otherwise, the game won't understand what you're trying to do.

Implementing Special Arguments in Commands

Sometimes, commands require you to know specific information about the world. For example, the `teleport` command doesn't work unless you enter the name of a player who's currently online — this can be quite impractical in a server where several players join and leave, especially when you want to teleport players via command block. Fortunately, there are a few versatile substitutes for common parameters that you can use to make your commands always work.

Examining relative positions

Many commands require you to enter coordinates as parameters, which can be cumbersome. For example, if you want to target a particular location, you have to press F3, record your coordinates, find the difference between your coordinates and those of the target location, and calculate the target location.

Relative positions are often easy to calculate, and they're useful for writing generalized commands. Essentially, if you precede a coordinate with a tilde (~), the coordinate is relative to the player or command block running the command. For example, if you enter the coordinates ~0 ~-1 ~0, the command interprets this as the space just below the player or command block. You can even use a single tilde in place of ~0, so you can, for example, use the command fill ~ ~ ~ ~ ~1 ~ gold_block to place gold blocks on both your position and the position just above you. Similarly, tp Isometrus ~5 ~3 ~ teleports the player Isometrus five blocks to the east and three blocks up from his original position.

Applying selectors

Much like relative positions, selectors are used to write general and versatile commands with many applications. They allow you to target players without knowing their usernames, target several players, and even target entities of all sorts (basically any nonblock object in the world, including creepers, minecarts, and fireballs).

If you right-click a command block, the screen that appears (refer to Figure 7-1) contains the following information about using selectors:

```
Use "@p" to target nearest player
Use "@r" to target random player
Use "@a" to target all players
Use "@e" to target all entities
```

You can use these selectors in place of any parameter that requests a target, such as a player. For example, if you use the command tp @r 0 64 0, a random player is teleported to the coordinates (0, 64, 0). However, if you type tp @e 0 64 0, every entity in the world is teleported there.

You can also add modifiers to a selector, making it target only certain entities. For example, @a[r=20] targets all players within 20 blocks, and @e[type=Zombie,c=3] targets three zombies. Every modifier takes this form:

```
[<argument1>=<value1>,<argument2>=
<value2>,. . .,<last argument>=<last value>]
```

If you apply this modifier, the selector targets every entity for which every argument is satisfied by the value given. To explain this, Table 7-3 lists the arguments you can apply, and which entities they accept.

Table 7-3	Selector Modifiers
Argument	*Use*
c	Limits the number of entities to target. For example, c=4 finds the first four entities, and c=-2 finds the last two.
l	Targets players with a certain maximum level.
lm	Targets players with a certain minimum level.
m	Targets players in a certain game mode. 0 is Survival, 1 is Creative, 2 is Adventure, and 3 is Spectator.
r	Targets entities within a certain range.
rxm, rx	Targets entities whose rotation about the x-axis is between the values given (clockwise from rxm, counterclockwise from rx).
rym, ry	Targets entities whose rotation about the y-axis is between the values given (clockwise from rym and counterclockwise from ry).
score_<name>	Targets players whose score in the objective is at most the given value. (<name> is an objective in the scoreboard; see the later section "Managing a Scoreboard.")
Score_<name>_min	Targets players whose score in the objective is at least the given value. (<name> is an objective in the scoreboard; see the later section "Managing a Scoreboard.")
team	Targets all players on the team (see "Managing a Scoreboard") whose team name matches the value provided.
name	Targets entities with a certain name. Entities with names include players (with their usernames) and mobs that were named (for example, with the Name Tag item).

(continued)

Table 7-3 *(continued)*

Argument	Use
type	Targets entities with a certain type, such as Player, Chicken, or PigZombie. You can find the different entity types by using the autocompletion feature on the summon command. (See the earlier section "Autocompleting Commands on the Chat Menu.")
x, y, z	Tests for entities at the target coordinates. Modifiers such as r and dx are centered at these coordinates.
dx, dy, dz	Tests for entities at most a certain distance away in the x, y, and z directions, respectively (thus searching for entities in a rectangular area).

Managing a Scoreboard

The last use of the command discussed in this chapter is managing the scoreboard. This feature allows you to record different variables and use them to modify your machines (for example, via the testfor command) or to display information to players. You can assign players to teams, manage achievements and statistics, and even adjust the game interface. This section introduces you to the functions of the scoreboard and to the commands used to activate them.

To use the scoreboard feature easily, it's immensely helpful to use the autocompletion feature. (See the earlier section "Autocompleting Commands on the Chat Menu.")

Creating scoreboard objectives

One of the most fundamental applications of the scoreboard is its ability to store *objectives,* or variables that store information about players. For example, you can have objectives that track players' health or show how much damage each player has dealt. You can even have an objective that can be incremented via command block whenever a player completes an achievement. This section deals with the scoreboard `objectives` command, which is used for creating and modifying objectives, but not their values.

The commands for objectives are as follows.

```
scoreboard objectives add <name>
<criteriaType> [display name ...]
```

In a new world, the scoreboard has no objectives and does essentially nothing. You use the `scoreboard objectives` command to add a new objective to the scoreboard. `<name>` is the name of the objective (cannot contain spaces). `<criteriaType>` is the type of objective you're creating, which can take the following values:

- `<any achievement or statistic name>`: Use the official name of an achievement or statistic (found via autocompletion) to track it with this objective.

- `deathCount`: Tracks the number of times the player has died.

- `dummy`: This command never updates itself — it's changed by command blocks, or players with cheating powers.

- `health`: Tracks the player's health. This is the only command that cannot be changed manually, and it changes only when the player's health changes. Health is measured in half-hearts, so a player with a full 10 hearts has a health value of 20.

- `killedByTeam.<color>`: Tracks the number of times the player was killed by a member of a team with a certain team color. For example, if a world is set up to be a fight between a red team and a blue team, members of the red team might have a `killedByTeam.blue` objective.

- `playerKillCount`: Tracks the number of players that the tracked player has killed.

- `teamkill.<color>`: The inverse of `killedByTeam`, tracks the number of kills the player has performed on players with a certain team color.

- `totalKillCount`: Tracks the number of mobs (including other players) that the player has killed.

✔ `trigger`: Like the dummy objective, can be changed only manually. However, even players without cheats can modify it, if given permission. (See the `enable` command in the next section.)

Lastly, [`display name`] is the name used whenever the objective is displayed. This name *can* contain spaces. If no display name is provided, the `<name>` is used instead.

Minecraft supports a wide range of characters, which is useful when making objectives look pretty. For example, I like to use `scoreboard objectives add HealthObj health ♥`.

    scoreboard objectives list

Lists all the objectives you've created, including their display names and types.

    scoreboard objectives remove <name>

Deletes the objective with a certain name (official name, not display name).

    scoreboard objectives setdisplay <slot>
    [objective]

Displays an objective in a certain place in the world. `<slot>` can take the following values:

✔ `belowName`: The objective's name and value are displayed beneath the name tags of players. You cannot see this objective above your own character — only other players.

✔ `list`: If you press the List Players button (Tab by default) you can see a list of all players on the server. If you use this objective display, the objective is displayed as a yellow number along with the player's name on the list. Note that with this setting, the objective's name is *not* displayed.

✔ `sidebar`: A menu appears at the side of the screen. The top of the bar shows the objective name, and each row contains a player name along with her score in that objective. The sidebar doesn't appear unless the objective has updated for at least one player.

✔ `sidebar.team.<color>`: A suboption of the preceding command, this one causes the objective to be displayed on the sidebar, but only to characters with the specified team color.

If an objective name isn't provided, the display slot is cleared so that any objective already there is removed.

Acquainting players with the scoreboard

After you create objectives, you can then modify their values. This is done via the `scoreboard players` command, which modifies the scores each player has in the objectives you've created. The commands are described in this section.

```
scoreboard players add <player> <objective>
<count> [dataTag]
```

Adds points to the player's score in a certain objective. <player> is the target, <objective> is the objective to modify, and <count> is the number of points to add. For example, if the nearest player has a score of 3 in the TotalDeaths objective, the command `scoreboard players add @p TotalDeaths 3` increases it to 6. The optional [dataTag] parameter is used to affect only players with particular data tags (see Chapter 10).

```
scoreboard players enable <player> <trigger>
```

Enables the target player to modify a trigger-type objective. This allows the player, whether or not he can cheat, to use the `trigger <objective> <add|set> <value>` command and modify the objective. (It works just like the add/set commands in this list.) This works well with the `tellraw` command, which allows players to execute commands with the click of a button.

```
scoreboard players list
```

Lists all players who are being tracked by the scoreboard.

```
scoreboard players operation <targetName>
<targetObjective> <operation> <selector>
<objective>
```

Changes a player's score with respect to another score. This might mean adding two scores together, or multiplying them, for example. The first two parameters specify the player and the objective to modify. `<operation>` can be +=, -=, *=, /=, or %=, which mean sum, difference, product, quotient, and remainder, respectively — this is the operation applied on the score. To decide what exactly you're adding or subtracting to the score, for example, specify another score with `<selector>` (choose the player) and `<objective>` (choose the objective).

```
scoreboard players remove <player>
<objective> <count> [dataTag]
```

Just like the earlier add command, removes points from a certain objective for the target players.

```
scoreboard players reset <player> [objective]
```

Completely wipes the score of the target player in the target objective. If no objective is specified, all of the player's scores are reset.

```
scoreboard players set <player> <objective>
<score> [dataTag]
```

Functions similarly to the earlier add and remove commands, except that it ignores the player's former score and sets it equal to the new input.

```
scoreboard players test <player> <objective>
<min> [max]
```

Similar to the testfor command, this command checks to see whether the target player has a score greater than `<min>` (and, if specified, less than `[max]`) in a certain objective.

You can type an asterisk (*) in place of any player selector for player and team commands — this allows you to target every player currently tracked by the scoreboard.

Creating teams with the scoreboard

The last feature of the scoreboard is creating teams of players and allocating players to them. This allows you to set up a lot of different settings specific to certain teams or team distribution.

You can create, delete, and modify teams with the commands in this section.

```
scoreboard teams add <name> [display name...]
```

Creates a new team with the name provided. When a team is first created, it doesn't contain any players. The optional [display name...] parameter allows you to display a different name than the team's official name — the display name can have whitespace.

```
scoreboard teams empty <team>
```

Removes all members from the team with the given name.

```
scoreboard teams join <team> <player>
```

The target player joins the target team.

```
scoreboard teams leave <player>
```

The target player leaves the team.

```
scoreboard teams list
```

Lists the names and display names of all teams, as well as the number of players in each one.

```
scoreboard teams option <team> <option>
<value>
```

Similar to the gamerule feature, this command allows you to change the settings of the target team. <option> can take the following values:

✔ `color`: Players on the team have their usernames changed to a different color.

✔ `deathMessageVisibility`: When a player on the team dies, this option decides whom to broadcast this news to on the Chat menu. `<value>` can equal `always`, `never`, `hideForOtherTeams`, or `hideForOwnTeam`.

✔ `friendlyfire`: `<value>` can be `true` or `false`. If it's set to `false`, players on this team can't harm each other directly.

✔ `nametagVisibility`: It decides whether the name-tags of players on the team are visible. `<value>` can equal `always`, `never`, `hideForOtherTeams`, or `hideForOwnTeam`.

✔ `seeFriendlyInvisibles`: `<value>` can be `true` or `false`. If it's set to `true`, players on this team can see invisible teammates as transparent images.

```
scoreboard teams remove <name>
```

Deletes the team with the given name.

Nonplayer entities can be added to the scoreboard, too (though their names appear as long strings of unintelligible alphanumeric characters). You can then use items such as zombies or fireballs to store these variables, for various purposes. The next few chapters help you understand the different ways you can use these commands.

8

Using Data Tags to Customize Objects

In This Chapter

- Understanding the structure of a data tag
- Implementing data tags in entities, items, and blocks
- Debugging broken data tags
- Using attributes, displays, and more to customize your game

A data tag is a variable stored in an object — that is, a block or an entity — taking various values that can affect how that object performs. When executing commands that summon, adjust, or detect these objects, you can include values of certain data tags to implement into the process. If you want to create chests with preset contents, zombies wielding powerful weapons, or giant stacks of chickens, you can do this and more with the right data tags. This chapter shows you how to use all sorts of data tags, and how to apply them to enhance your Minecraft experience in creative new ways.

Understanding the Syntax of Data Tags

Data tags are described in a special language that is added to normal commands. For example, take a look at this command:

```
summon Creeper ~ ~ ~ {powered:1b,
    ExplosionRadius:9}
```

This command works as written — the curly brackets and colons are all necessary. The command summons a creeper as it should, but the {powered:1b,ExplosionRadius:9} segment provides the creeper with some special settings that determine how it acts.

In general, a set of data tags takes the following form:

```
{tag1:value1,tag2:value2, ...,
    lasttag:lastvalue}
```

Essentially, each tag is the name of an attribute, and the corresponding value is how you want the attribute to be defined. In this command example, powered and ExplosionRadius are both tags, and 1b and 9 are their respective values.

Each tag, depending on its type, can take different sorts of values. For example, a tag might take a string of text as a value to record an entity's name, or it might take a number that determines how much health the entity has. This is what makes them so powerful — almost any tag can be edited with commands, which means that you can tinker with the innermost mechanics of any block, item, or entity. If a value is ineligible for a tag, your command won't function as intended.

The different types of tags are described in this list:

- **String:** A length of text. For example, {id:Silverfish} or {Command:say Hello World} are both eligible data tags — the id and Command tags accept strings as values, and the values provided satisfy this requirement. You must use quotation marks for strings that contain commas or curly brackets.

- **Short:** A short number (less than 4096). You often must add a lowercase *s* to the value — for example, {Fuse:200s}.

- **Int:** A number less than 2147483648; just like short tags, but with a much greater range.

- **Byte:** A very small number; less than 256. Because bytes have a slightly different format than other numbers, you often have to add a lowercase *b* to the value — for example, {inGround:1b}. Many bytes can take only two values: 0 (false) and 1 (true). These values are often referred to as *booleans*.

✔ **Long:** An extremely long number. These variables are often used automatically by Minecraft and are rarely applied by players.

✔ **Float:** Short for *floating-point variable,* these values can be decimals. Though it can also be an integer, a float variable must contain a decimal point somewhere, even if it's something like "1.0." Floats often must end with a lowercase *f* — for example, {FallHurtAmount:0.5f}.

✔ **Double:** The most versatile numerical input, a double can be any integer or decimal within an extremely large range (up to 2^{1024}, which is over 300 digits long) — for example, {Base:123.45}.

✔ **List:** Some values are lists of other values — this means putting several values in a bracketed list, separated by commas. For example, you could use {DropChances: [0.0f,1.0f,1.0f,1.0f,0.5f]} to record a list of five float values.

✔ **Compound:** Lastly, some values are data tags themselves. They may represent entities, blocks, or special objects such as attributes. They're formatted just like other data tags. For example, {Riding:{id:Slime,Size:5}} is a data tag within another data tag.

You do not have to implement every possible data tag. If you don't specify a tag, the computer will set it for you.

When using data tags, you may have to write very long commands. Some of the fun commands are too long to fit inside a single line on the Chat menu, so many of the tools to follow cannot be applied in this way. Remember to put long commands into command blocks (which have virtually no length limit), or else they may be cut short.

To implement data tags into a command, you simply have to place the compound (everything inside curly brackets, as shown in the earlier examples) into the proper space. To see how data tags are implemented in various commands, see Chapter 7.

Introducing Data Tags Belonging to Entities

Most entities can take many different data tags that affect their status, abilities, resources, and behaviors. The different entity data tags available are described in Table 8-1.

Table 8-1		Entity Data Tags
Tag	*Value*	*Effect*
Any Entity		
Air	Short	Indicates how many ticks (20ths of a second) the entity can hold its breath underwater before it begins to take damage. This tag equals 300 when the entity's breath is full.
CustomName	String	A name given to the entity, which displays instead of its normal name if specified.
CustomName Visible	Byte	If equal to 1, the entity's custom name (see the preceding description) is displayed over its head. If equal to 0, the name is displayed only if the player is nearby and looking directly at the entity.
FallDistance	Float	The distance the entity has fallen. If you set this value manually, you can increase the damage that occurs when the entity hits the ground.
Fire	Short	If this tag is not equal to –1, the entity is not on fire. If it's positive, it indicates the number of ticks (20ths of a second) that the entity spends on fire.

Tag	Value	Effect
Invulnerable	Byte	If this tag is set to 1, the entity cannot be damaged or destroyed except by players in Creative mode. Otherwise, the tag is set to 0.
OnGround	Byte	This tag equals 1 when the entity is on the ground, and equals 0 otherwise.
Portal Cooldown	Int	The number of ticks (20ths of a second) before the entity is allowed to travel through a portal.
Pos	List	Contains three doubles representing x-, y-, and z-coordinates.
Motion	List	Contains three doubles representing x-, y-, and z-velocity.
Riding	Compound	A fun tag that allows the entity to sit on top of any other entity. The value of this tag is a data tag for the entity being ridden — it must contain the ID tag to specify what type of entity it is. For example, try this command: `summon Slime ~ ~ ~ {Size:0,Riding:{id: Slime,Size:1,Riding:{id: Slime,Size:2}}}`
Rotation	List	Contains two floats representing rotation about the y- and x-axes.
Any Nonplayer		
id	String	The type of entity. You can find the names of entities by autocompleting the `summon` command (see Chapter 7).
Arrow		
InData	Byte	The metadata value of the block that the arrow is in (the short number determining the block's variant).

(continued)

Table 8-1 *(continued)*

Tag	Value	Effect
life	Short	Counts up from 0 when the arrow isn't in motion and returns to 0 if the arrow moves. If it reaches 1200 ticks (20ths of a second), the arrow is destroyed.
pickup	Byte	If 0, the arrow cannot be picked up. If 1, the arrow can be picked up. If 2, the arrow can be picked up only in Creative mode.
Bat		
BatFlags	Byte	When equal to 1, indicates that a bat is hanging on the underside of a block.
Byte		
SkeletonType		If equal to 1, the skeleton is a wither skeleton.
Cats and Dogs		
Sitting	Byte	Equal to 1 if the animal is sitting down.
Creeper		
Explosion Radius	Byte	The radius of the blast created by the creeper when it explodes.
ignited	Byte	If equal to 1, the creeper has been ignited with flint and steel and is about to explode.
powered	Byte	If equal to 1, the creeper is surrounded by a bright blue aura and produces a much larger explosion.
Creeper or Activated TNT		
Fuse	Short	The number of ticks (20ths of a second) it takes for the entity to explode.
Donkeys and Mules		
ChestedHorse	Byte	If equal to 1, the donkey or mule is carrying a treasure chest.

Tag	Value	Effect
Items	List	The items carried by the entity. It's a list of items (see the section "Implementing Data Tags in Items," later in this chapter). Every item compound must contain the Slot tag, specifying which inventory slot the item is in (must be at least 2 for animals because 0 and 1 are the saddle and armor slots).
Dropped Item		
Age	Int	The number of ticks (20ths of a second) the item has been left uncollected. When it counts up to 6000, the item is destroyed. You can set Age to −32768 (negative 2 to the 15th power) to prevent it from counting.
Owner	String	If the name of a player is specified for this tag, only that player can pick up the item. If the item is 10 seconds away from disappearing, anyone can pick it up.
PickupDelay	Short	Indicates the number of ticks (20ths of a second) before the item can be picked up. This tag does not count down if initially set to 32767 (2 to the 15th power, minus 1).
Thrower	String	If the item was dropped by a player, Thrower records the player's name.
Dropped Items and Item Frames		
Item	Compound	The item represented or contained by the entity. See the later section "Implementing Data Tags in Items" for more on item compounds.

(continued)

Table 8-1 *(continued)*

Tag	Value	Effect
Enderman		
CarriedData	Short	A data value determining the variant of the block carried by the enderman. For example, can specify a specific color of wool.
Endermite Count	Int	The number of endermites spawned by the enderman. If set to 15 or higher, no more endermites will spawn.
Carried	Short	The ID of the block that the enderman is carrying.
Endermite		
Lifetime	Int	Indicates the number of ticks (20ths of a second) the endermite has lived, up to its death at 2400.
Firework		
FireworksItem	Compound	The item corresponding to the firework entity. Must include the tag "id:fireworks." See the later section "Creating custom fireworks" to see how to set the tags for this item.
Life	Int	The number of ticks (20ths of a second) for which the rocket has been flying.
LifeTime	Int	When the firework's Life tag (see the preceding description) reaches this value, it explodes. You can create an instant explosion by summoning a firework with LifeTime less than or equal to Life.
Ghasts and Fireballs		
Explosion Power	Int	The radius of the blast created by a ghast's fireballs; can be attributed to both ghasts and the fireballs themselves.

Tag	Value	Effect
Guardian		
Elder	Byte	If equal to 1, the guardian is an elder guardian.
Horse		
ArmorItem	Compound	The armor being worn by the horse (see the later section "Implementing Data Tags in Items").
Eating Haystack	Byte	Equal to 1 while the horse is eating.
SaddleItem	Compound	The saddle being worn by the horse (see "Implementing Data Tags in Items").
Tame	Byte	Equal to 1 if the horse is tame. If equal to 0, it throws off any entity riding it.
Temper	Int	Determines how easy the horse is to tame, from 0 to 100.
Type	Int	The type of horse (0 = normal, 1 = donkey, 2 = mule). You can also summon horses that don't normally appear in the game, such as the zombie horse (3) and skeletal horse (4).
Variant	Int	The color and markings on the horse. Each color is associated with an integer, starting with 0 — the same is done for patterns. To choose the variant of a horse, take the color ID and add 256 times the pattern ID.
Iron Golem		
PlayerCreated	Byte	If equal to 1, the iron golem is aligned with the players.

(continued)

Table 8-1 *(continued)*

Tag	Value	Effect
Item Frame		
ItemDrop Chance	Float	The probability that the item frame will drop its contents when destroyed, between 0.0 (never) and 1.0 (always).
ItemRotation	Byte	The rotation of the item within the frame, from 0 (upright) to 7 (rotated 315 degrees clockwise, or 45 degrees counterclockwise).
Item Frames and Paintings		
Facing	Byte	Represents which way the entity is facing. Can be 0, 1, 2, or 3 (clockwise from south).
TileX, TileY, TileZ	Int	These three tags represent the coordinates of the block that the entity is attached to.
Livestock		
Age	Int	A value that always counts toward zero in ticks (20ths of a second). Babies have negative Age and become adults once the counter hits zero. Adults increase the counter after breeding and cannot do so again until the counter returns to zero.
ForcedAge	Int	When a baby animal grows up, its Age value (see the preceding description) is set equal to this value.
InLove	Int	The number of ticks (20ths of a second) during which the animal looks for another of its same species.

Tag	Value	Effect
Minecart		
Custom DisplayTile	Byte	If equal to 1, show a certain block inside the minecart (though the block doesn't do anything). The block is determined by the DisplayTile tag explained next.
DisplayTile	String	The name of a custom block shown inside the minecart. Only shows if the CustomDisplayTile is equal to 1. If you use a custom block, you can also use the tags DisplayData and DisplayOffset, ints that determine the ID of the block's variant (starting from 0) and the distance between the block and the minecart (in 16ths of a block).
Minecart with Furnace		
Fuel	String	The number of ticks (20ths of a second) before the minecart loses power and stops accelerating on its own.
PushX, PushZ	Double	The two tags that determine the acceleration of the minecart (velocity of increase in velocity) in the x- and z-directions. You can observe these variables with things such as the `testfor` command, but you cannot modify or set them yourself with commands such as `summon`.
Mob		
Absorption Amount	Float	Amount of bonus health given to the mob (this health cannot be restored when lost).

(continued)

Table 8-1 *(continued)*

Tag	Value	Effect
ActiveEffects	List	A list of compounds describing the effects currently placed on the mob. Each compound contains up to five tags: the mandatory byte *Id* (the ID of the effect, see Chapter 7), the byte *Amplifier* (number of times the effect is upgraded), the int *Duration* (length of the effect), and the zero-or-one bytes *Ambient* and *ShowParticles* (determines whether the particles are transparent and visible, respectively). For example, a mob with two different effects might look like: `{ActiveEffects: [{Id:1,Amplifier:3, Ambient:1},{Id:12, Duration:100000}]}`
CanPickUp Loot	Byte	Equal to 1 if the mob can pick up items and equip armor lying on the ground. Otherwise equal to 0.
DropChances	List	A list of five floats, representing the chance that the defeated mob will drop its equipment. The floats refer to (in order) the item that the mob carries, its boots, leggings, chestplate, and helmet. Each chance is a number between 0.0 and 1.0. For numbers greater than 1.0, the mob's equipment always drops and does not lose durability. This does not work unless the mob's equipment (described next) uses a Count tag, like `{Count:1}`.

Tag	Value	Effect
Equipment	List	A list of five compounds representing the mob's equipment. The five compounds are (in order) the item that the mob carries, its boots, leggings, chestplate, and helmet. Mobs can wield any item and wear any item on their heads (often with humorous results). Each compound is a set of data tags for an item — see the section "Implementing Data Tags in Items," later in this chapter.
Leash	List	If the mob is leashed to a fence post, this is a list of three integers specifying the coordinates of the post.
Leashed	Byte	If equal to 1, the mob is leashed to a block or entity determined by the Leash tag (see the preceding description).
Persistence Required	Byte	If equal to 1, the mob does not go away until it is defeated. Because mobs naturally "despawn" in Minecraft, this is useful for creating important entities.
HealF	Float	The mob's health (possibly a decimal). Cannot exceed the mob's maximum health.
Mobs, Dropped Items and XP Orbs		
Health	Short	The mob's health — cannot exceed its maximum health. This tag is overridden if HealF is specified, so it is often safer to modify HealF instead (see the preceding entry).
Ocelot/Cat		
CatType	Int	The type of cat. Can be 0, 1, 2 or 3, corresponding to Ocelot, Tuxedo, Tabby, and Siamese, respectively.

(continued)

Table 8-1 *(continued)*

Tag	Value	Effect
Painting		
Motive	String	The name of the artwork shown on the painting. At the time of this writing, the possible names are: Alban, Aztec, Aztec2, Bomb, BurningSkull, Bust, Courbet, Creebet, DonkeyKong, Fighters, Graham, Kebab, Match, PigScene, Plant, Pointer, Pool, Sea, Skeleton, SkullAndRoses, Stage, Sunset, Void, Wanderer, Wasteland, and Wither.
Pig		
Saddle	Byte	Equal to 1 if the pig is saddled.
Players and Villagers		
Inventory	List	A list of items (see "Implementing Data Tags in Items") in the entity's inventory. Items in the player's inventory must include the Slot tag, specifying which slot the item is in.
Projectile		
InGround	Byte	Equal to 1 if the projectile is grounded, and 0 if it is in the air.
InTile	String	The name of the block that the entity is in.
xTile, yTile, zTile	Short	These three tags represent the coordinates of the projectile in its "chunk," or 16-x-16 region. You generally don't need to mess with these values.
Sheep		
Color	Byte	The color of the sheep's wool. There are 16 different colors, which correspond to the values from 0 to 15.

Tag	Value	Effect
Sheared	Byte	Equal to 1 if the sheep has been sheared.
Slimes and Magma Cubes		
Size	Int	The size of the slime; 0 is the smallest. Very large slimes may slow down your game.
Thrown Potion		
Potion	Compound	The data tags representing the thrown potion (see the later section "Implementing Data Tags in Items").
Thrown Projectile		
ownerName	String	The name of the player who threw the projectile.
Villager		
Profession	Int	A number corresponding to the color of the villager's clothing. IDs begin at 0.
Riches	Int	The total number of emeralds that have been sold to the villager.
Willing	Byte	If equal to 1, the villager is willing to have children.
Wither		
Invul	Int	This tag counts down to 0 in ticks (20ths of a second). During this time, the wither is invulnerable. Though the counter has a large value, the wither's body appears invisible.
Wolf		
Angry	Byte	Equal to 1 if the wolf is angry.
CollarColor	Byte	The color of the wolf's collar. There are 16 different colors, which correspond to the values from 0 to 15.

(continued)

Table 8-1 *(continued)*

Tag	Value	Effect
XP Orb		
Value	Short	The number of experience points provided by the orb.
Zero-Gravity Projectiles		
direction	List	A list of three doubles determining the direction of the fireball, small fireball, or wither skull.
Zombie		
CanBreak Doors	Byte	Equal to 1 if the zombie can break down wooden doors. Otherwise, equal to 0.
Conversion Time	Int	If the zombie is slowly turning back into a normal villager, this value represents the number of ticks (20ths of a second) before the zombie turns. Otherwise, the value is set to −1.
IsBaby	Byte	Equal to 1 if the zombie is a zombie baby.
IsVillager	Byte	Equal to 1 if the zombie is a zombie villager.
Zombie Pigman		
Anger	Short	The hostility of the monster toward the player. If a zombie pigman has an anger of 0, it is completely neutral unless provoked.

Integrating attributes and modifiers in entities

You can also use data tags to change an entity's *attributes,* certain variables that determine its behavior. You can do this with the Attributes tag, a somewhat complicated tag in the form of a list of compounds. You can modify many attributes, with interesting effects.

The data tag is written as follows (this can be placed alongside other tags or put directly into a command, just like other tags — see the following example):

```
{Attributes:
[
    {Name:<name1>,Base:<base1>},
    {Name:<name2>,Base:<base2>},
    {Name:<name3>,Base:<base3>},
    ...
    {Name:<last name>,Base:<last base>}
]
}
```

The Modifiers tag applies to each element in the list, which is a list of modifiers to the attributes that don't change the attributes' base values. However, this is used mostly for internal calculations, and when summoning entities, you really only need to manipulate the attributes themselves.

This can be difficult to understand at first, but it becomes simpler when you examine it piece by piece. Essentially, the Attributes tag is a list of attributes, each of which is a compound detailing the attribute's name (see Table 8-2, at the end of this section) and value.

Suppose that you run this command:

```
summon Zombie ~ ~ ~ {Attributes:
    [{Name:generic.maxHealth,Base:100},
    {Name:generic.knockbackResistance,
    Base:1.0},
    {Name:generic.followRange:200}]}
```

This command summons a zombie that has three specialized attributes:

- ✔ **It has 100 hit points,** because of the {Name:generic.maxHealth,Base:100} tag.

- ✔ **It cannot be knocked back by attacks,** because of the {Name:generic.knockbackResistance,Base:1.0} tag.

- ✔ **It chases players who are very far away,** because of the {Name:generic.followRange:200} tag.

Such an enemy would probably make a good "boss battle" in a custom map (see Chapter 10).

Table 8-2 describes each attribute. Every attribute in the table should be written into the command as it is displayed.

Table 8-2	Attributes for Entities
Attribute	*Effect*
generic.attackDamage	The damage dealt by the mob with physical attacks. (Fireballs and the like are not affected, but melee and archery are.)
generic.followRange	The mob must be at least this many blocks close to a target in order to pursue it.
generic. knockbackResistance	The probability that a mob is not knocked back by an attack. The number must be a decimal between 0 (no chance) and 1 (always).
generic.maxHealth	The mob's maximum hit points.
generic.movementSpeed	The mob's speed. Make this a small number — 0.7 is default, and 1 is very fast.
horse.jumpStrength	The height to which a horse can jump. The default is 0.7, and the maximum is 2.
zombie. spawnReinforcements	The chance that the zombie summons another zombie when attacked. The number must be a decimal between 0 (no chance) and 1 (always).

Summoning customized villagers

Another interesting use of entity data tags is the ability to customize villagers. *Villagers* are mobs that can trade items with players, and their trading options are usually generated randomly. However, by customizing a villager with data tags, you can specify exactly what the villager wants to buy and sell.

For example, you can make a villager trade an emerald for a diamond, red wool for blue wool, gold nuggets for enchanted armor, a wooden sword and a stone sword for an iron sword, and so on. This is useful for creating shopkeepers with very specific settings, such as a villager who accepts lapis lazuli in different quantities in exchange for weapons and potions. You can give villagers as many trading options as you want, and they can trade absolutely any item you want.

The tag is written this way:

```
{Offers:
    {
       Recipes:
         [
            <recipe1>
            <recipe2>
            . . .
            <last recipe>
         ]
    }
}
```

Each recipe is a compound that can contain the following tags:

- **buy:** An item compound (see "Implementing Data Tags in Items," later in this chapter) representing the item that the villager wants to buy.

- **buyB:** An item compound representing another item that the villager wants to buy. (Villagers sometimes want two different items in exchange for their wares.)

- **maxUses:** The maximum number of times the trade can be used. This can be set to an extremely large number if you want the trade to be nearly infinitely available.

- **rewardExp:** Equal to 1 (by default) if you gain experience points by using this trade. Otherwise, equal to 0.

- **sell:** An item compound representing the item that the villager wants to sell.

- **uses:** The number of times the trade has been used. This defaults to 0, so you generally can keep it as is.

Thus, for example, you could program a villager by entering the following command:

```
summon Villager ~ ~ ~ {Offers:{Recipes:[{
    buy:{id:diamond,Count:50},
    sell:{id:diamond_sword,tag:{ench:[{id:16,
       lvl:6}]}}
    },{
    buy:{id:planks},buyB:{id:emerald},
    sell:{id:iron_block},maxUses:999999,
       rewardExp:0}
]}}
```

This command creates a villager with two different offers:

✔ The first trade allows you to spend 50 diamonds
(buy:{id:diamond, Count:50}) in exchange for a
diamond sword with the Sharpness VI enchantment.
(sell:{id:diamond_sword,tag:{ench:[{id:16,
lvl:6}]}})

✔ The second trade allows you to spend wooden planks and
an emerald (buy:{id:planks},buyB:{id:emerald})
in exchange for an iron block (sell:{id:iron_block}),
but does not grant experience points (rewardExp:0) —
this trade also almost never expires, because it can be
used 999999 times (maxUses:999999).

Throwing blocks around with the FallingSand entity

You may recall that sand and gravel blocks fall if there are no
blocks underneath to support them. While one of these blocks
is falling, it temporarily turns into the FallingSand entity,
before turning into a block again when it lands. However, the
addition of data tags to the game marked a huge change in the
usefulness of these entities — namely, you can make an entity
out of *any* block and drop it onto the world.

The FallingSand entity has tags that can change which block
it represents, what it does when it falls, and even which data
tags the block has. For example, you can throw a chest into
the air so that it lands, damages anyone it hits, and fills itself
with a particular arrangement of items. You can discover
unlimited possibilities by turning blocks into entities like
this — get creative!

If you summon a FallingSand entity without data tags, it disappears almost instantly. If you want to summon it properly, set the Time tag to equal at least 1, indicating that the entity exists.

In addition to the tags in Table 8-1, the tags available to FallingSand entities are described in this list:

- **Block:** The name of the block represented by the entity.

- **Data:** An integer determining the variant of the block being used (for example, wool color) with 0 being the default.

- **DropItem:** A byte equal to 1 if the block should drop an item when mined by a player.

- **FallHurtAmount:** If the HurtEntities tag equals 1, this number is proportional to the amount of damage that entities receive when the block falls on them.

- **FallHurtMax:** If the HurtEntities tag equals 1, entities cannot take more than this amount of damage when the block falls on them.

- **HurtEntities:** A byte equal to 1 if the entity should cause damage to whatever it lands on. Damage is proportional to how far the entity had fallen.

- **TileEntityData:** A compound containing all the tags that will be related to the block.

- **Time:** The number of ticks (20ths of a second) for which the entity has existed.

For example, consider the following command:

```
summon FallingSand ~ ~1 ~ {
Motion:[0.0,0.5,1.5],
Block:command_block,Time:1,HurtEntities:0,
TileEntityData:{
CustomName:Aerial Commander,Command:
    say Hello World
}
}
}
```

This command produces a command block that is launched across the horizon and, when it lands and is powered, produces this message:

```
[Aerial Commander] Hello World
```

Equipping and posing armor stands

Armor stands are wooden sculptures that can equip armor and wield items—and with the right data tags, they can be posed and set up any way you want, creating sculptures and scenes of any sort.

Locking the equipment of armor stands

One problem with armor stands is that players can freely mess with its equipment. Fortunately, this can be controlled with the `DisabledSlots` tag. This tag accepts an integer as input — depending on the value of this tag, certain parts of the stand cannot be removed, replaced, or modified. For example, if you use the command `summon ArmorStand ~ ~ ~ {DisabledSlots:2096896}`, a stand is created that cannot be modified. To figure out which integer you have to use, follow these steps:

1. **Choose an armor slot to disable.**

   Each one corresponds with a number: 1 for the wielded item, 2 for boots, 4 for leggings, 8 for chestplate, and 16 for helmet.

2. **Decide whether to disable removing, replacing, or adding an item in that slot.**

   If you picked replacing, multiply the number by 256. If you picked adding, multiply the number by 65536. Use a calculator, if necessary.

3. **If you want to disable multiple options, repeat Steps 1 and 2, and then add the numbers together.**

   For example, if you want an armor stand such that neither a helmet nor boots can be added to it, your number is 1048576+131072=1179648. You can add together as many numbers as you want this way.

Setting some general properties of armor stands

Some data tags help you design your armor stands, and offer some interesting features that you can apply, as described in this list:

- **Equipment:** A compound of five items (refer to the identical tag in Table 8-1), which determines what the armor stand is wearing and wielding.

- **Invisible:** If equal to 1, the armor stand is invisible, only showing its equipment. For example, you could put a block over an invisible armor stand's head so that it appears as a block suspended in the air.

- **NoBasePlate:** If equal to 1, the stone base of the armor stand is invisible.

- **NoGravity:** If equal to 1, the armor stand can float in midair.

- **ShowArms:** If equal to 1, the armor stand has little wooden arms.

- **Small:** If equal to 1, the armor stand is much smaller, and its equipment shrinks to match.

Posing your armor stand

One more important feature of the armor stand is that every single joint can be rotated. You can do this with the Pose tag, which in turn contains up to six data tags: Body, LeftArm, RightArm, LeftLeg, RightLeg, and Head. Each one of these tags is a compound of three floats between -360 and 360, indicating its rotation about the x-, y-, and z-axes. For example, if you enter the command summon ArmorStand ~ ~ ~ {Pose: {Head:[30.0f,0.0f,0.0f]}}, your armor stand will be looking down at the ground. Similarly, if you enter the command summon ArmorStand ~ ~ ~ {Pose:{LeftLeg:[30. 0f,0.0f,0.0f],RightLeg:[0.0f,0.0f,60.0f]}}, your armor stand will appear to be dancing awkwardly.

Implementing Data Tags in Items

In addition to entities, items can have data tags. These data tags allow you to customize the features and properties of an item, which is useful for creating powerful swords, items that can break only certain blocks, items with descriptions, and more.

Items are often used as arguments in other data tags. If a data tag takes an item as its value, the item tag should take this form:

```
{id:<item name>,Count:<# of items>,Slot:<slot
   where item is>,Damage:<damage value of
   item>,tag:<other data tags>}
```

Only the `id` tag is always mandatory, but other tags may be required, depending on the context. When using commands such as `give`, you don't need to structure items in this way, because everything besides `tag` is already specified in the other arguments of the command.

Table 8-3 shows the different tags available for items (excluding the ones just mentioned).

Table 8-3		Data Tags for Items
Tag	*Value*	*Effect*
Any Item		
CanDestroy	List	A list of the names of blocks that the item can destroy. If a player is wielding this item in Adventure mode, she can destroy any of the blocks named in this list.
ench	List	A list of all the enchantments on the item. Each enchantment is expressed as a two-element compound containing the id tag (ID of the enchantment, starting at 0) and the lvl tag (level of the enchantment). For example, to get Sharpness III and Flame I, the tag would be `{ench:[{id:16,lvl:3}, {id:50,lvl:1}]}`

Tag	Value	Effect
HideFlags	Int	If this integer is positive, certain parts of the item's tooltip (which appears when hovering the cursor over the item or item name) are hidden, if they aren't hidden already. If equal to 1, enchantments are hidden. If equal to 2, attribute modifiers are hidden. If equal to 4, the Unbreakable trait is hidden. If equal to 8, the list of blocks it can destroy is hidden. If equal to 16, the list of blocks it can be placed on is hidden. If equal to 32, all other nonessential information is hidden. If you want to hide more than one of these things, take all the corresponding numbers and add them together.
RepairCost	Int	When the item is modified with an Anvil, the value of this tag is added to its cost.
Block		
BlockEntity Tag	Compound	If an item can be placed in the world as a block, this compound is a set of tags that are given to the new block. See the later section "Containing Data Tags in Blocks."
CanPlaceOn	List	A list of the names of blocks on which that the item can be placed. If players are wielding this item in Adventure mode, they can place it on any of the blocks named in this list. For example, you can make it so that a button can be placed only on a diamond block.
Book		
author	String	The book's author.

(continued)

Table 8-3 *(continued)*

Tag	Value	Effect
Enchanted Book		
Stored Enchantments	List	A list of all enchantments contained by the book. When the book is combined with another item, these enchantments are transferred to it. The tag works just like the ench tag (described earlier in this table).
Items with Durability		
Unbreakable	Byte	If equal to 1, the item does not lose durability when used.
Map		
map_is_scaling	Byte	Equal to 1 if the map is scaled, such that each pixel on the map represents multiple blocks. This value cannot be changed, only tested with commands such as `testfor`.
Mob Head		
SkullOwner	String	The username of the player represented by the head. You can also use MHF_ followed by certain strings to produce special heads — this includes most mob names, certain blocks (Cactus, Chest, Melon, OakLog, Pumpkin, TNT, TNT2) and some symbols (ArrowUp, ArrowDown, ArrowLeft, ArrowRight, Question, Exclamation). For example, I can use the tag `{SkullOwner:MHF_Sheep}` to create a little cubical figurine of a sheep. Works only if the skull's data is 3.

Tag	Value	Effect
Potion		
CustomPotion Effects	List	A list of compounds representing each effect the potion produces when you drink or throw it. For instructions on these compounds, refer to the description of the ActiveEffects tag in Table 8-1.
Written Book		
generation	Int	Indicates how many times the book has been copied from the original. For example, 0 is the original, and 2 is a copy's copy. If equal to 3, the book is marked as tattered.
pages	List	A list of strings, with each string representing one page of the book. You can use JSON-style text here, like you do with the `tellraw` command (see Chapter 7) — this means you can make books with colored text, clickable text, and more without using mods.
title	String	The title of the book.

Modifying attributes through items

Table 8-2 (earlier in this chapter) shows some special variables, called attributes, that make entities function differently. You can manipulate these with items as well — by adding attribute *modifiers* to an item, it can change the attributes of the enemy wearing or wielding it. This means that both players and other entities can have their attributes changed simply by holding an item. (For players, this means selecting the slot containing your item with the 1–9 keys or the scroll wheel.)

Modifiers add a value or percentage to a certain attribute, and a single attribute can have several modifiers. To implement these, you must use the AttributeModifiers tag. This tag is a list of compounds, with each compound representing a modifier.

Each compound in AttributeModifiers contains the following fields:

- **Amount:** The number to add or multiply, for example, to the attribute. It can be negative or a decimal, if you want.

- **AttributeName:** The name of the attribute (refer to Table 8-2).

- **Name:** A name associated with the modifier. You can choose any string you want — whereas AttributeName requires an official name from Table 8-2, this Name tag is just for documentation purposes.

- **Operation:** Determines how Amount is used to modify the attribute. It can take the following values:

  - *0:* The value of Amount is added to the attribute. For example, if an attribute has a value of 5 and Amount equals 2, the attribute then becomes 7.

  - *1:* The attribute is multiplied by a value determined by Amount. For example, if Amount is 0.5, the attribute gets a +50 percent bonus. When several of these modifiers are used, the percentage bonuses are added up — if two modifiers both have Amount equal to 0.5 and Operation equal to 1, the total percentage bonus is 50% + 50% = 100 percent.

  - *2:* Just like 1, this operation adds percentage bonuses to the attribute — however, when several of these modifiers are used, they are handled a bit differently. Rather than the percentage bonuses being added together, they're applied in succession. For example, two 50 percent bonuses add up to a 125 percent bonus (1.5 times 1.5 equals 2.25), not a 100 percent bonus, like Operation 1 does.

  When multiple modifiers are used at one time, those with Operation equal to 0 are always calculated first, and those with Operation equal to 2 are always calculated last.

- **UUIDLeast and UUIDMost:** These two numbers, when collated, form a unique identity for the Modifier. Though these are mandatory, you don't need to worry about them much — just select any two numbers, and don't let two modifiers have the same UUID if they modify the same attribute.

For example, this command produces a magical diamond that causes several effects to whoever holds it:

```
give Isometrus diamond 1 0
 {AttributeModifiers:
[
    {AttributeName:generic.maxHealth,Amount:5,
       Operation:0,Name:Health+,UUIDLeast:999,
       UUIDMost:999},

    {AttributeName:generic.
       maxHealth,Amount:0.5,Operation:1,
       Name:Healthx,UUIDLeast:999,
       UUIDMost:1000},
    {AttributeName:generic.attackDamage,Amount:
       -1,Operation:0,Name:No Damage,UUIDLeast:
       999,UUIDMost:999},

    {AttributeName:generic.movementSpeed,
       Amount: 2,Operation:1,Name:Superspeed,
       UUIDLeast: 999,UUIDMost:999}
]
}
```

If something is holding this diamond, the following things happen to the entity:

- ✔ **Its health is increased by 5, and then increased by 50 percent.** This is done through the first two modifiers. Structures such as this are helpful for creating balanced effects for entities with any base number of hit points.

- ✔ **Its damage is reduced.** In fact, a player cannot attack at all while holding the diamond, because it reduces his base damage from 1 to 0.

- ✔ **Its movement speed is tripled.** If a player holds the diamond, she can turn off this effect by switching to a different inventory slot.

Figure 8-1 shows a player who is holding this diamond, and the various effects it causes.

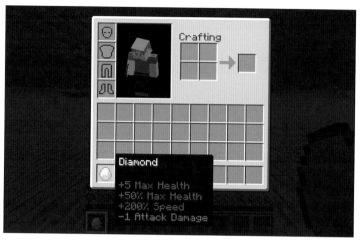

Figure 8-1: Examining attribute modifiers on a diamond.

Implementing the display tag

Items also use the moderately complex display tag, a compound tag containing some options for the more aesthetic capabilities of items. The display tag can contain the following subtags:

✔ **color:** If your item is a piece of leather armor, this tag can be used to change its color. You can choose from more than 16 million possible colors, and each one is associated with a number. To find this number, you must follow these steps:

　1. *Record how much red you want, as a number between 0 and 255.*

　　0 doesn't include any red in your color, and 255 includes a lot of red.

　2. *Repeat Step 1 for green and blue.*

　　Computers create colors from mixtures of red, blue, and green. If all three are 0, the color is black, and if all three are 255, the color is white. Also note that red and green make yellow in computer-speak.

　3. *Multiply the red number by 65536, and multiply the green number by 256. Leave the blue number as is.*

You need a calculator for this part, preferably one that accepts eight-digit numbers.

4. Add together the red, blue, and green numbers.

The result is the number that represents the color you chose!

✔ **Name:** A string representing the name of the item. You can change this string to name items whatever you want.

✔ **Lore:** The "lore" of an item is a number of lines of text that can show beneath the item's name. The Lore tag is a list of strings, with each string representing a line of text.

For example, consider the following command:

```
give Isometrus leather_leggings 1 0 {display:
    {color:32894,Name:Jeans of Power,Lore:
    ["Damage absorbed in lifetime:",]}}♥♥♥
```

This command creates a blue piece of armor with a customized tooltip, as shown in Figure 8-2.

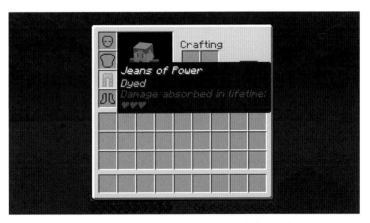

Figure 8-2: Using data tags to elaborate on a normal piece of armor.

Creating custom fireworks

Another complex item tag structure is the firework. Fireworks can produce many customizable particle effects, and unlike with the `particle` command, you can customize their colors and other visual settings.

Each firework rocket contains the Fireworks tag, a compound containing a byte called Flight, and a list called Explosions. Flight is the number of seconds before the rocket detonates — unfortunately, you cannot make the rocket detonate instantly unless you summon its entity directly. (See the earlier section "Introducing Data Tags Belonging to Entities.") Explosions is a list of more compounds, representing every explosion the firework makes when it detonates. Thus, the Fireworks tag should always take this form:

```
{Fireworks:{Flight:<byte>,Explosions:[<list>]}
```

Each explosion compound in `<list>` can be customized with the following tags:

- **Colors:** A list of every color to appear in the firework. Every color is represented by an integer. (To find this integer, see the section "Implementing the display tag," earlier in this chapter.)

- **FadeColors:** This is just like the Colors tag, except that it determines all colors that the original colors fade out to as the firework dissipates. For example, you could make a blue-and-green firework that fades into yellow and green near the end of the effect.

- **Flicker:** Equal to 1 if the explosion has a twinkling effect.

- **Trail:** Equal to 1 if the explosion has a trailing effect.

- **Type:** A byte representing the sort of blast you're creating. 0 is a small ball (default), 1 is a large ball, 2 is a star, 3 is in the shape of a creeper face, and 4 is an upward burst.

For example, take a look at the following command:

```
give Isometrus minecraft:fireworks 1 0
{Fireworks:
{Flight:1,Explosions:[
{Colors:[16711680,16744448],FadeColors:
   [16776960]},
{Colors:[16776960],Type:1,Flicker:1}
]}}
```

This command summons a firework that explodes after one second, creating a twinkling yellow outer layer and a red-and-orange inner layer that fades into the same yellow (see Figure 8-3).

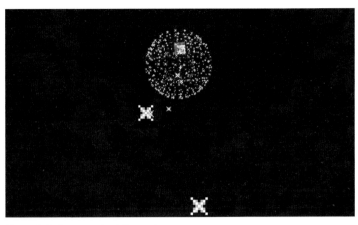

Figure 8-3: A customized firework.

You can also program Firework Stars in this way, using the Explosion tag (which contains the compound for a single explosion) instead of the Fireworks tag.

Containing Data Tags in Blocks

Data tags can even be implemented in blocks. Often referred to as Tile Entities because, like entities and unlike items, they have a physical existence in the world, many blocks have the capacity for customized data tags. Table 8-4 shows the data tags available to blocks. Block-specific tags are grouped together.

Table 8-4	Data Tags Available to Blocks	
Tag	*Value*	*Effect*
Any Block		
id	String	The name of the block.
x, y, z	Int	These three tags represent the x-, y-, and z-coordinates of the block, respectively.

Table 8-4 *(continued)*

Tag	Value	Effect
Beacon		
Levels, Primary, Secondary	Int	The first tag is the beacon's level. The Primary and Secondary tags are the IDs of the two effects that the beacon provides. See Chapter 7 to find effect IDs.
Brewing Stand		
BrewTime	Int	Records the number of ticks (20ths of a second) for which the contained potions have been brewing.
Command Block		
Command	String	The command that is activated when the command block is powered.
LastOutput	String	The text shown in the command block's Previous Output box.
SuccessCount	Int	If the command block is running a testing command such as `testfor`, this variable represents the signal strength that the command block provides to adjacent comparators.
Containers		
Items	List	A list of all items in the container. The item compound must include the Slot tag, specifying which slot the item is in. (See "Implementing Data Tags in Items," earlier in the chapter.) If the container is a furnace, Slot 0 is the item being cooked, Slot 1 is the item used as fuel, and Slot 2 is the output.

Tag	Value	Effect
Containers and Beacon		
Lock	String	If specified, a player cannot open this container unless she is holding an item with the same name as the lock. This must be a _custom_ name — for example, a lock named "Diamond" cannot be opened with a diamond, but rather an item custom-named "Diamond."
Containers, Enchanting Table, and Command Block		
CustomName	String	If specified, this string is displayed in the container menu rather than the block name. For example, a custom-named chest could show as "Jacob's Wooden Sword Stash" rather than "Chest."
Flower Pot		
Data	Int	If the flower pot contains a plant, this tag's value represents the variant of the plant. The default variant is 0, and other variants are represented as 1, 2, 3, and so on.
Item	String	The name of the plant contained in the flower pot.
Furnace		
BurnTime	Int	The number of ticks (20ths of a second) for which the furnace's fuel lasts before another fuel item must be consumed.
CookTime	Int	The number of ticks (20ths of a second) during which the current item has been cooking. An item is fully cooked when this tag's value reaches 200 ticks (10 seconds).

(continued)

Table 8-4 *(continued)*

Tag	Value	Effect
Hopper		
Transfer Cooldown	Int	The number of ticks (20ths of a second) before the hopper can transfer its contents to another container. Whenever the hopper makes a transfer, this tag is set to eight ticks.
Jukebox		
RecordItem	Compound	The item contained in the juke-box. See the earlier section "Implementing Data Tags in Items."
Note Block		
note	Byte	The note being played by the note block, in half-steps (0 is F#, 1 is G, 2 is G#, and so on). Has a maximum of 24 (two octaves up).
Piston		
blockData	Int	The data value determining the variant of the block that the piston is pushing.
extending	Byte	Equal to 1 if the piston is extending or retracting its arm.
facing	Int	Indicates the direction the piston is facing — 0 is down, 1 is up, 2 is north, 3 is south, 4 is west, and 5 is east.
progress	Float	If the piston is in the process of pushing or pulling, this value indicates how far it is through the animation (0.0 initially, 1.0 when finished).

Tag	Value	Effect
Redstone Comparator		
OutputSignal	Int	The strength of the current going through the comparator.
Sign		
Text1, Text2, Text3, Text4	String	The text contained in each of the four lines on the sign. You can implement text in JSON form (the sort of text used with the `tellraw` command, as explained in Chapter 7).
Skull		
Owner	Compound	If the skull has type 3, this compound describes the player whom the skull represents. This includes the UUID tag (a long string of characters uniquely identifying the player) and the Name tag (the player's username).
Rot	Byte	A number from 0 to 15 indicating the direction in which the skull is facing.
SkullType	Byte	A number representing what type of skull it is. 0 is skeleton, 1 is wither skeleton, 2 is zombie, 3 is player, and 4 is creeper.

An entity such as Minecart with Chest or Minecart with Hopper can implement all the same tags as the item it contains. The Minecart with Furnace is an exception because it uses the furnace in a unique way.

A block which is particularly Mob spawners are blocks that appear in various naturally generated structures, having the ability to summon entities around them. These blocks have several features that can make them more versatile than even the summon command:

 ✔ **They can summon entities conditionally on the number of nearby entities.** Spawners can pause before they overload the world with entities.

✏ **They can activate based on the proximity of players.**
Spawners can function only if a player is within a suitable
distance from it. This is always the case, but data tags
can be used to change the parameters of this effect.

✏ **They can summon random selections of entities.** A
single spawner can summon random entities in random
group sizes at random intervals.

✏ **They can be destroyed in Survival mode.** For example,
when building a custom map (see Chapter 10), you could
have it so that players must fight through an infinite
horde of enemies to reach and destroy their source.

Mob spawners have a number of different tags that allow you
to customize how they perform their function:

✏ **Delay:** The number of ticks (20ths of a second) before
the spawner creates entities. The counter pauses when
the spawner is out of players' range (see SpawnRange,
later in this list). It can be set manually, so you can create
a spawner with a Delay of 0 to summon entities as soon
as the player draws near.

✏ **EntityId:** The name of the first entity to be spawned. If
SpawnPotentials is not defined, this spawner continues
to create this entity.

✏ **MaxNearbyEntities:** The largest possible number of
entities near the spawner before it pauses work. Only
detects entities of the same type as those summoned by
the spawner. The radius by which "nearby" is defined is
about twice the spawner's SpawnRange.

✏ **MinSpawnDelay, MaxSpawnDelay:** The spawner waits
some number of ticks between each summoning — this
number is chosen randomly from between MinSpawnDelay
and MaxSpawnDelay.

Always make MaxSpawnDelay positive, or else the game
will overload trying to process an infinite number of
actions at one time. It's okay to set MinSpawnDelay equal
to 0, though.

✏ **RequiredPlayerRange:** The proximity (in blocks) that
the spawner must be to a player in order to function.

✏ **SpawnCount:** A short variable that determines the maximum number of entities it can spawn at a time.

✔ **SpawnData:** A set of data tags to attribute to the entity from the EntityId tag.

✔ **SpawnPotentials:** A list of all possible entities that can be spawned. You still have to define EntityId even if you use this tag — EntityId defines the first entity to be spawned, and SpawnPotentials defines all the rest. SpawnPotentials is a list of compounds, and each compound has these tags:

- *Type:* The name of the entity.

- *Weight:* An integer proportional to the entity's chance of being summoned. For example, if a spawner has two potential entities, one with a weight of 1 and one with a weight of 2, the latter is summoned twice as often as the former.

- *Properties:* A compound of the data tags belonging to the entity.

The original entity, defined by EntityId, has a weight of 1 in this probability distribution.

✔ **SpawnRange:** The maximum horizontal distance (in blocks) from the spawner in which the entities can be spawned. Vertical distance cannot be changed — entities will spawn directly above, next to, or below the spawner if a space is available. Note that the space in which entities can be spawned is square, not circular.

If your spawner isn't working the way you want, specify some more tags. The more specific you make its purpose, the more likely it is that it will perform it correctly. Also try closing and reopening the world or switching to a different version of Minecraft, if the spawner looks like it should be working but simply isn't.

For example, the following command summons various entities under different conditions:

```
setblock ~ ~1 ~ mob_spawner 0 replace {
EntityId:Enderman,MaxNearbyEntities:5,
    RequiredPlayerRange:3,
Delay:0,MinSpawnDelay:30,MaxSpawnDelay:120,
    Spawn Count:1,
SpawnRange:3,
SpawnPotentials:[
{Type:Endermite,Weight:80},
```

```
{Type:Silverfish,Weight:20,Properties:{
    CustomName:Megamite}}
]
}
```

When the player draws near, an enderman is instantly summoned, and then the spawner begins creating endermites, some silverfish, and occasionally another enderman.

 If you specify the Pos tag on an entity summoned by a spawner, you can decide exactly where the entity appears — even outside the spawner's range.

Fixing Bugs in Commands and Their Data Tags

You can easily make mistakes when composing data tags. Further, these mistakes can be difficult to locate. This section describes some techniques you can use whenever your commands don't work, in order to discover and fix the problem.

Trying out some general debugging methods

If a command just doesn't work, you can try a few things that apply in many cases:

- **Remove some tags.** Use cut-and-paste (Ctrl-X and Ctrl-V) to temporarily remove some of the tags you're using. If the problem goes away, there's a bug in the tags you removed. If the problem doesn't go away, there's a bug in the tags you didn't remove, or a problem with the command in general. You can apply this strategy to narrow down the tags that are causing errors in your command.

- **Check the type of values passed to your data tags.** Some tags require strings of text, and others require numbers within a certain range, and so on. Be sure to check the tables in this chapter to make sure you're using your tags properly.

✔ **Watch out for extra brackets, curly brackets, quotation marks, and colons.** Especially if you use a tag that takes strings as input, make sure that there are no characters that might be misinterpreted. For example, the colon in the string "Effect: +2 Health" may confuse the compiler unless you enclose the entire string in quotation marks, indicating that it's a string and not a misused tag.

Identifying specific error messages

If these tactics don't work, you may have to look at the specific error message displayed in the command block's Previous Output text box. If you click on this error message and scroll to the beginning by pressing the Home key, you can see why exactly the command block is having a problem with your input.

9
Combining Commands

In This Chapter

- Applying command blocks together to produce interesting results
- Integrating command blocks into redstone circuits
- Designing generalized commands

*T*he commands detailed in Chapter 7 can help you accomplish many interesting tasks — however, many people combine these commands with circuits or other command blocks to produce the effects they want. This chapter is all about implementing command blocks in machines, in order to discover new and limitless innovations.

Discovering the Applications of Combined Commands

Every command block is associated with a single function — however, you are by no means limited to one function at a time. Many programs (redstone or otherwise) use multiple functions at a time, sometimes putting many functions together in large circuits.

Figure 9-1 shows a simple example of using multiple commands at one time: when the lever is flipped, a platform is created, a powerful mob appears on top of the platform, and the mob begins periodically producing particle effects and throwing splash potions in all directions.

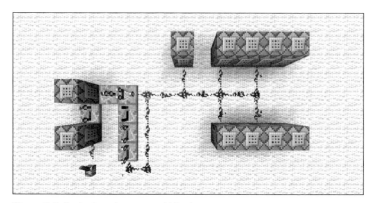

Figure 9-1: A cluster of command blocks.

By combining functions in this way, you can produce elaborate programs that change the way you play Minecraft.

Exploring interesting command-block combinations

To get started using combined commands, you may want to try combining a few command blocks, running them all at once or in sequence. The following list provides some groups of commands that go well together — it's up to you to decide what the inputs for the commands should be:

- ✓ effect + effect clear

  Give a player an effect (like Haste or Absorption, something that changes the player's capabilities), and then clear the effect whenever you want later on.

- ✓ execute + particle + playsound

  Produce a particle effect and play a sound when an entity executes a command.

- ✓ gamemode + clear + spreadplayers

  Reset players' positions in a world by assigning them to a game mode, clearing their inventories, and spreading them around a certain starting point.

✔ gamerule + gamerule + gamerule

It is often efficient to set all game rules with a single lever or button, for example.

✔ replaceItem + replaceItem + replaceItem

By adding, removing, or rearranging many items in a chest or inventory, you can redistribute an entity's items or revise the contents of containers.

✔ setblock + setblock + setblock

Sometimes, changing a single block isn't enough to make an impact on your world.

✔ say + any command

Some commands are rather important, so you may want to notify players in chat when those commands are executed.

✔ tell + any command

If a command pertains to only one player, you can tell that player when the command is executed.

✔ title + any command

If a command is especially important, you can notify players of that command in large letters.

✔ scoreboard players add + give + xp

Grant items and/or experience points whenever you give points to a player.

✔ tellraw + trigger

One command gives players the ability to execute commands by way of chat; the other ensures that the players are given temporary access to these particular commands.

Connecting command blocks and comparators

Some commands are *made* to be linked with other devices, producing little to no effect on their own. At the time of this writing, these commands are testfor, testforblock, and testforblocks.

Figure 9-2 shows an example of command blocks connected by comparators. The command blocks at the top execute this command:

```
testfor @a[score_Checkpoint=<X>,score
    Checkpoint_min=<X>]
```

The command blocks at the bottom execute these commands:

```
Scoreboard players set @a Checkpoint <X>
effect @a 21 1000000 <X> true
```

In these commands, <X> is replaced by 1, 2, 3, 4, or 5, depending on which column the command block is in. When the lever is flipped, all players are given the Health Boost effect with power equal to the highest achieved Checkpoint score.

Figure 9-2: Using conditional command blocks.

The following list describes other commands that benefit from connections with testfor, testforblock, and testforblocks:

✔ blockdata

Fill a chest with items if a certain requirement is satisfied, or modify a block if it contains the correct data tag. (See Chapter 8 for more on data tags.)

✔ clear

A popular technique in command block programming is using an item in a player's inventory, such as a key, to activate an ability or a function. For example, if you use the testfor command and discover that a certain item is in the player's inventory, you can remove that item and use it to execute a command.

✔ clone

This command works particularly well with testfor blocks: You can check for a certain arrangement of blocks and, if you find it, move or copy it to another location.

✔ effect

Provide effects to the player based on certain restrictions. For example, a testfor circuit could give players a short jump boost whenever they stand over a group of blocks.

✔ execute

If testfor finds that certain entities share a particular quality, you can use the execute command to run any command with respect to each of those entities.

✔ fill

It's useful to check for certain blocks or entities before filling an area with blocks.

✔ give

Don't just give items to players anytime — you can provide tools and rewards when players achieve a certain score on the scoreboard, have another item to give in exchange, or place a certain block in a certain location.

✔ kill

Inflict swift punishment on certain actions, such as entering a certain area or dealing too much damage to other players.

✔ particle and playsound

Use visual elements and sound effects to indicate the results of your test command.

✔ `replaceItem`

Add, remove, or change the item in a certain slot whenever a certain condition is satisfied.

✔ `say`, `tell`, or `title`

Broadcast the results of your test command.

✔ `scoreboard`

The features of the scoreboard, as explained in Chapter 7, work well with these commands. See the following sections for examples of how to use it.

✔ `setblock`

Change a certain block as long as a certain condition is satisfied. For example, if a certain `testfor` argument succeeds, you can place a redstone block elsewhere in the world and activate a circuit in another location.

✔ `summon`

Summon an entity only when the circumstances are right.

✔ `tellraw` and `trigger`

`trigger` allows players to execute commands when they normally couldn't — unfortunately, this command works only for certain scoreboard commands. Fortunately, if a player uses a trigger command in this way, you can use `testfor` to detect it and execute another command of your choice. This works well with `tellraw`, a command commonly associated with triggers (see Chapter 7).

✔ `tp`

Teleport players and entities conditionally. For example, teleport all players to the center of a room if one of them steps out of bounds.

✔ `worldborder add`

Increase or decrease the size of the world border when a player obtains a certain score or when a certain block is modified.

✔ `xp`

Grant experience points to players in response to certain restrictions being met.

If you want something like testforblock to function relative to an entity (for example, to check the block directly above the entity or a few blocks to the side), use the execute...detect command instead. This useful double command executes an action relative to an entity only if a certain space contains a certain block. While rather complex, this command is explained fully in Chapter 7.

Using the scoreboard to combine commands

The scoreboard is one of the most useful features to integrate with commands. As explained in Chapter 7, you can use the scoreboard to assign a set of variables to each player and then manipulate and display those variables.

Here are some examples of ways you can implement your scoreboard in command block designs:

- **Measure and modify statistics.** For example, you could have an objective named Weaponsmith that tracks the statistic stat.craftItem.minecraft.diamond_sword. You might then grant the player an item when the objective reaches a certain value or add to the objective whenever a weapon-upgrading machine is used.

- **Use objectives as currency.** Try this combination of commands: If a player's objective exceeds a certain value, reduce it by that value and give the player a reward. Whether the objective represents money, skill points, or keys, it can represent an expendable resource that the player trades for practical gain.

- **Use objectives to represent progression.** Suppose that you have a machine for challenging players with increasingly difficult waves of mobs. You might create a waveNum objective to track which wave the players are on, making a command block to increase it by 1 and connecting it to the wave-running device. Then you can have the machine summon only powerful mobs such as skeletons when, say, waveNum exceeds 5. This system is also useful for telling players the wave number — just display waveNum on the sidebar, or with a command such as say or title.

✔ **Use teams to distribute and distinguish players.** Use a command that adds a player to a certain team when activated — then other commands can be set to affect only players on a certain team.

Applying Commands to Redstone Machines

In Creative mode, command blocks aren't just a substitution for the circuits explained in the first half of this book. Command blocks activate whenever they're powered by redstone current — thus, when linked into a redstone circuit, they can function in interesting ways. See the following sections for different ways to integrate command blocks and circuits.

Creating impossible machines with command circuits

Sometimes, redstone circuits simply cannot perform certain functions. For example, you can't transmit information remotely, you can't complete complex algorithms in a short time, and many machines have to be at least a certain physical size. The addition of command blocks can help you ignore most of these restrictions.

Commands can execute many different functions to manipulate any part of the world, making them much more versatile than the circuitry tools available in Survival mode. Here are some ways you can improve your circuits with command blocks:

✔ **Create more complex input and output.** Command blocks can change the world in many different ways — use this to your advantage! Instead of pushing blocks with pistons, use the `clone` tool to move entire platforms in otherwise unimaginable ways. Rather than use simple iron doors, build beautiful walls that crumble in multicolor explosions with the push of a button. When using command blocks, never feel limited by the constraints of normal redstone circuits.

✔ **Use command blocks to modify the components of a circuit.** Command blocks can rotate redstone repeaters, place redstone blocks, and more with the `setblock` command. For example, if you want a circuit to activate a device elsewhere, just place a redstone block next to the device.

✔ **Use command blocks to store memory, not memory latches.** The memory latch, explained in Chapter 5, is useful for storing a single bit of information (or more, if you string together multiple memory latches). However, command blocks make this process much easier — whether you use entities, blocks, or scoreboard objectives, command blocks can produce and store information that can easily be accessed by the circuit (usually via `testfor` or `testforblock`).

Figure 9-3 shows what a circuit might look like when implementing command blocks. Note that space efficiency hardly matters any more: The pieces of the circuit are simply put together in a way that best reflects how the program is structured. Because command blocks can affect any part of the world without the need for connections, everything in the figure can be part of a single circuit.

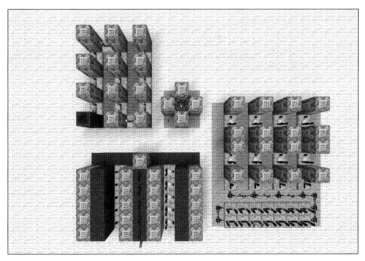

Figure 9-3: A large command block program.

Setting command blocks on loops

One particularly useful way to implement a command block is on a loop. This makes the command block activate over and over, which can have some interesting results. Many commands have to be repeated in order to unlock some of their deeper applications, and this section gives you a few examples of such commands.

Before working with the concepts in this section, I suggest that you execute the `gamerule commandBlockOutput false` command first. This command turns off the messages that appear on the Chat menu whenever a command block activates, and it prevents the Chat menu from becoming overloaded with repetitive notices.

Some looped commands can be hazardous to your world. For example, summoning hordes of dragons can cause massive lag, and rapidly teleporting players can block off their access to the world completely. To avoid an apocalyptic faux pas, be sure to give cheating privileges only to players you trust, and make backups of your world (copy and paste all corresponding folders) before you attempt any risky maneuvers.

Some of the commands that work particularly well inside loops are described in this list:

✔ `clear`

Placing this command on a loop can slowly drain a certain item from players' inventories or prevent players from holding that item in their inventory altogether.

✔ `execute`

It is useful to make a player or a mob or another entity execute a command every now and then. You can give players fun effects, create powerful enemies with special abilities, and even make a bow that leaves a trail of slime when fired.

✔ `give`

You can make a player's items return over time after they're used or give players bonuses at regular intervals.

✔ `particle`

Sometimes, special effects don't last long enough for your purposes. Put this command on a loop and you can produce these effects repeatedly, or even continuously.

✔ `playsound`

Play sounds at different intervals to produce some ambient background sounds.

✔ `say`

Display periodical notices or warnings.

✔ `scoreboard`

You can have fun looping plenty of scoreboard commands. You can change the sidebar display to slowly cycle between a few objectives or rapidly increase a player's score like a stopwatch, for example.

✔ `setblock`

By repeatedly setting a certain space in the world to a certain block, you can produce some interesting results, especially if you do so with part of a circuit.

✔ `summon`

Sometimes, a single entity isn't enough to provide a sufficient function or challenge. Swarms of entities are often much more interesting. A block that constantly summons entities can be handy, whether you're creating mobs or items. Don't overdo it, though — a large number of complex entities can slow down the game.

✔ `tellraw`

This command provides messages with many different functions, so it is often useful to ensure that the player always has access to these sorts of messages.

✔ `testfor`, `testforblock`, `testforblocks`

These commands are extremely useful when looped. You can rapidly check for a certain parameter and, when it's met, execute a command or circuit.

✔ tp

Teleport an entity to a certain position every once in a while. Teleporting players repeatedly this way has some uses, but can often be irritating.

You can teleport mobs and the like by using the tp command.

✔ xp

Many players like to rewrite the Experience bar to act as a customized gauge. If you do this, you can put this command on a loop to make players' experience points gradually increase by rapidly adding a constant. This constant can be negative, making experience points slowly deplete.

Using Generalized Variables to Create Commands Efficiently

Command blocks can do so many things that time constraints are often the only limitations. Sometimes, a program requires many different command blocks, and these sometimes take a while to design, place, and write out. This section shows you ways to make outstanding command block designs that take little time to build and require hardly any repetitive work.

Using one command block in place of many

Used correctly, a single command block (or, at most, a few) can do the work of many others. This section describes a few techniques for making your command blocks as time- and space-efficient as possible:

✔ **Use** fill **and** clone, **not** setblock. If you want to put the same block in many different locations, just use the fill command a few times. For example, if you want to make a large, hollow square from obsidian, just fill a square shape with obsidian blocks and then fill a square inside it with air.

In addition, if you want to place a certain arrangement of blocks in one or more locations, build that arrangement somewhere out of sight, and then clone it to the appropriate destinations. These two methods can save you the trouble of searching for lots of different coordinates and writing dozens of setblock commands or more.

✔ **Use** scoreboard players operation **to make programming much easier.** This command allows you to add one scoreboard objective to another. Thus, don't use tons of scoreboard players add commands to make a variable behave the way you want — store some other objectives to draw information from.

✔ **If you have to use many command blocks, all with similar commands, remember to copy and paste.** Press Shift+Home or Shift+End to quickly select large chunks of code, and press Ctrl+C and Ctrl+V to copy and paste them. Alternatively, press Ctrl+A to select an entire command at one time. This technique is useful for writing a bunch of commands that are, for the most part, equivalent.

Mastering relative coordinates

Another useful technique when managing command blocks is using relative coordinates. As explained in Chapter 7, when using commands that require you to enter coordinates or angles of rotation, you can precede any number with a tilde (~) to make it relative. This number is then calculated as though the command runner were at the coordinates (0, 0, 0). For example, if a command block runs a command at ~ ~1 ~, it targets the block just above it.

Figure 9-4 shows an example of using relative coordinates to make this process much easier. The command block shown in the figure is loaded with the following command:

```
fill ~-2 ~ ~ ~-17 ~ ~ command_block 0 replace
    {Command:clone ~ ~ ~1 ~ ~ ~1 -1156 64 552
    replace}
```

When the command activates, it fills the empty spaces to its right with command blocks, each of which has the same command. When any of the pressure plates is triggered, the color of the wool block at the top changes to whichever one the player is in front of. This example shows how relative coordinates can make the same command do very different things, depending on the place from which the command is being executed.

Figure 9-4: A color-changing machine, managed by a single command block.

Using command block minecarts

Another way to simplify command block machines is with minecarts. A command block minecart can roll around a track and run a command any time it hits an activator rail, allowing it to easily execute its command from different places at different times.

However, note an even more important characteristic of minecarts with command blocks: They are not blocks — they're *entities*. Therefore, you can teleport minecarts, make them invisible or invincible, and place them in such a way that they don't affect blocks or other entities.

Figure 9-5 shows a block-jumping game where the player has a gauge made of diamond blocks to track his progress.

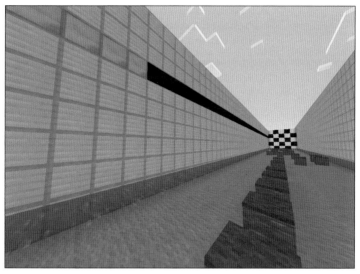

Figure 9-5: Dynamically monitoring a player's progression along a line.

You can use a single command block minecart to make this gauge to keep track of the player's progress. Just follow these steps:

1. **Place activator rails behind the gauge.**

   Set the rails on redstone blocks so that they're constantly active.

2. **Set the player onto a team.**

   This step allows commands to tell the difference between the player and whatever spectators happen to be in the world. Suppose that the team is named Runner — to create and fill this team, use these two commands, in order:

   ```
   scoreboard teams add Runner
   scoreboard teams join Runner <player
        name>
   ```

3. **Summon an invisible, indestructible command block minecart, equipped with the following command:**

   ```
   setblock ~ ~ ~1 diamond_block
   ```

4. Create a loop that rapidly teleports the minecart between the player and the corresponding activator rail behind the gauge.

First, you can teleport it to the player with this command:

```
tp @e[type=MinecartCommandBlock]
   @p[team=Runner]
```

Then you can teleport it to the gauge with this command (substitute your own y- and z-coordinates as needed):

```
tp @e[type=MinecartCommandBlock] ~ 10 712
```

Thus, the command block is constantly checking the player's position and landing on the activator rails to mark it.

10

Building a Custom World with Redstone

In This Chapter

- Understanding custom worlds
- Engineering for an audience
- Constructing rules and challenges for players
- Managing an adventure

*S*ome Minecraft players enjoy adventuring and monster-slaying more than building and construction — other players build worlds that offer them this experience. Because Minecraft worlds are stored in individual files that can be copied, shared, and downloaded between players, some players craft special worlds that contain interesting places, challenges, and adventures that invite other players to download and explore their worlds. These worlds have to be downloaded online or accessed through a server address, but there are tons of websites and forums through which players can share their creations for others to download and experience.

This chapter shows you some ways to use redstone (particularly the command block, as explained in Chapters 7 and 8) to construct these worlds.

Introducing Custom Worlds

Building custom worlds for other players is an interesting art — each custom world is a game in itself, despite being a subset of Minecraft. Custom worlds can consist of adventures, puzzles, survival challenges, or even variations of Minecraft that add new complications and settings. Figure 10-1 shows a player fighting his way through an adventure world that was created by someone else.

Figure 10-1: An adventurer locked in a preplanned battle.

These worlds (often referred to as *maps* or *custom maps*), come in many different forms, including

- **Structure showcase:** Some custom maps contain cities, interesting circuitry, or even entire player-generated continents, which other players can download and explore.

- **Challenge:** Some worlds contain custom challenges for players to try. These challenges may include puzzles powered by redstone, collections of blocks that the player must jump across, or groups of monsters to fight.

- **Adventure:** Particularly detailed worlds give players a story to follow and tasks to complete. These worlds are built to cleverly guide players through various environments and challenges while giving them items to use and opponents to overcome. Designers can even make use of Adventure mode, putting their players in a situation where they can't just break through walls and derail the game plan.

✔ **Minigame:** Some worlds involve only a small field or arena in which players can play minigames where they survive waves of monsters, throw snowballs at targets, or compete against each other. Minigames often use redstone power to manage the games and set up the components.

✔ **Minecraft variation:** Some maps place players in a world where they survive and build, as in a normal Minecraft game — with some additions. The world might have strange composition and architecture to make the game more intensive with extra dangers and challenges, or players may be given extra settings or resources to help them survive.

Customizing a Map for Other Players

To design a detailed custom map, make the map well-adjusted for your players: it should be sufficiently fun, not too easy or difficult, and well-detailed. In the following sections, I explain how to set up a map and use redstone to control the adventure.

Setting up the map

Especially in adventure or survival maps, be sure to complete these actions:

✔ **Set the world spawn.** This area is the one in which all new players first appear. Provide some sort of plaza or platform, and then use the setworldspawn command at its center to mark it.

✔ **Determine the game rules.** The gamerule command is important in determining the settings for the world. Many custom maps activate the keepInventory rule, and deactivate rules like doDaylightCycle, doMobSpawning, doTileDrops, doFireTick, and mobGriefing.

✔ **Give players proper freedoms and restrictions.** Players must be able to play your custom map, but don't let them break the mechanics of the game! Remember that every block in Minecraft can be destroyed. To prevent your brilliantly designed dungeon or arcade from being wrecked, you can use the defaultgamemode command to put all players in Adventure mode — this mode prevents players from breaking blocks unless they have the right tools, so you can choose exactly which tools they're allowed to have.

Bedrock and barriers make good walls for non-Adventure mode maps because they cannot be destroyed or moved by players, unless the game is in Creative mode.

✔ **Build that setting and instructions.** Players need to know where they are, how they should use the map, and what to do next.

Setting up the game is, relatively speaking, the easy part — you need to execute only a few commands from the Chat window, setting all the rules and modes detailed in the preceding list. After players have started on your custom map, however, you need to guide their actions to produce fun results. This is where the heart of your world's redstone takes effect, as described in the next section.

Controlling the adventure with redstone

As mentioned previously, redstone is meant to connect input to output — in a custom map, the inputs are the actions of the map's players. As players progress through the map, you can use redstone to control the adventure in various ways, including

✔ **Introduce redstone-powered challenges:** For example, hook some sticky pistons to a loop, which produces a set of constantly moving blocks that you can make players jump across or dodge. You can also use command blocks, or dispensers containing monster eggs, to summon enemies whenever players draw near.

✔ **Control minigames:** Do you want a game to have a scoring system? Do you want your minigame to complete computations to determine the challenges and rewards it gives to players? Do you want pistons to drop the losing player into the void? Most minigames like these use quite a bit of redstone behind the scenes, like circuits which control the mechanisms, or counters which record the players' scores.

✔ **Run scoreboards and variables:** You can use memory latches (see Chapter 5) or scoreboards (see Chapter 7) to keep track of the status of the map and players, from scores to progression to unlocked rewards. This sort of tracking is useful for creating a sense of completion for players, as long as you show them their progress along the way.

✔ **Create tricky blocks and entities with commands:** Maybe you want players to fight a spider-riding zombie with triple health or you want blocks and treasure chests to appear from nowhere with particular settings. You can do all this by connecting command blocks to pressure plates or other machines and by using the command to summon special blocks or entities.

✔ **Choreograph effects and events:** You can hook up redstone around the entire map to control its structure and progression — see the next section.

Using Redstone to Produce Coordinated Events

Whether you're managing a minigame or guiding an adventure, redstone engineering can be quite useful for making your custom map progress the way you like. Use input from players to run your programs and execute the events that occur on the map.

For example, Figure 10-2 shows three rooms of a custom map, with redstone linked around them. The redstone, which causes various monsters and rewards to activate, is activated by levers (which the players must use to open the doors) and hoppers (which players can throw items into). This arrangement ensures that players are faced with the proper challenge for each room, and must make certain payments (dropping particular items into the hopper) in order to get better rewards.

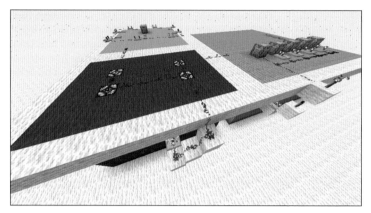

Figure 10-2: Redstone is connected between three rooms, marked in red, blue, and green.

A couple of interesting engineering problems may crop up when you create a redstone-powered map, as described in the following two sections.

Performing tasks determined by active player input

The machines you build for your map often have to see what players are doing in order to provide them with a good experience. The map can directly ask for the players' input — for example, set the players behind a locked door, requiring them to flip a lever. Then you can connect the lever to a hidden machine that players must activate to pass through the door.

You can gather active player input in a few different ways:

- **Basic levers, buttons, and pressure plates:** These are often the simplest and most popular ways to gather player input. For example, players can click a button to indicate that they're ready to continue or step on a pressure plate to activate an event.

- **Containers:** The redstone comparator can provide output proportional to the contents of a container, which means that your redstone machines can activate by simply having a player drop a "key" into a hopper (see Chapter 6 for filtering items with hoppers) or removing all items from a treasure chest.

✔ **Special chat messages:** You can use the `tellraw` and `trigger` commands (see Chapter 7) to send clickable messages to players, which allows players to activate other commands.

✔ **Just asking:** If you ask players to walk to a location or fight an enemy — via a chat message, a sign, or a hint, for example — you can turn passive input into active input: In other words, it turns absentminded decisions into ones that players are actively aware of. Players can then more easily understand their obligations, and you can more easily show them how the custom map should be experienced.

Figure 10-3 shows a tricky example of active player input: a store. Each button corresponds to a different reward. A player who presses the button — and who can pay the price of the item (determined by using scoreboards or other types of counters) — receives an item.

Figure 10-3: A shop that runs on active player input.

Triggering events with passive player input

Sometimes you don't want players to know everything that's going on, or you want to maintain a pure experience for them while working out the semantics yourself. In this case, you can use *passive player input* (actions without the intent of directly providing input to the controller) to silently keep the map working around them. For example, if a player walks into a room, you can use a hidden sensor to summon a boss battle. Or, if a player steps over a checkpoint in a racing game, you can use a tripwire to broadcast the player's achievement and alert other players to her progress.

You can collect passive player input in several ways:

- **Pressure plates and tripwires:** You can guide players into these traps fairly easily — for example, by using a low ceiling so that they can't jump over the trigger. If a pressure plate or tripwire is activated, the redstone recognizes that a player is in the right place and can respond by starting a machine, granting a reward, or summoning monsters, for example.

- **BUDs:** Block update detectors (see Chapter 5) are useful for detecting actions that players may believe are harmless. The trapped chest can also achieve this effect.

- **Timers:** Sometimes you might want machines to activate while players are just watching and waiting or while they're trying to complete a task. You can do this by stringing together redstone repeaters (see Chapter 2), which act as delays. Performing many events in a sequence, separated by set lengths of time, is useful for choreography, minigames, and battles with interesting complications.

- **The** `testfor` **command:** If you put a command block on a loop and have it repeatedly activate the `testfor` command (which searches for particular entities and provides proportional output to nearby comparators), you can test for players around a certain location. If you test for other entities instead, you can use the `testfor` command to see whether players have, for example, defeated all monsters in a room. This is useful for providing paths and rewards only after a challenge is complete.

In addition, the `testfor` command works well with the scoreboard. Note that scoreboard objectives can represent many different variables, from health to deaths to any achievement or statistic. You can then test for players with a certain score and use those results in interesting ways. For example, in Figure 10-4, there's a command block hidden five blocks beneath the player with the command `testfor @p[r=5]`. If this command block is repeatedly powered by a redstone loop (see Chapter 5), it waits until the player is at the center of the room and then powers a bunch of other command blocks which that surround the unsuspecting player with creepers.

Figure 10-4: Using passive input to produce interesting effects.

If you build lots of machines that respond to passive input, you can make your custom map feel almost like a *mod* (a program that adds extra content to the game). With some clever programming, you can essentially rewrite the rules of the game.

Constructing Challenges

Building minigames and adventures requires not only a fundamental understanding of redstone engineering but also a strong sense of game structure and design. Just as you might plan out a circuit or machine, challenges require some careful organization of mechanical tasks.

The following sections provide some tips and tricks for assembling challenges in your map.

Planning out and assembling a minigame

Minigames are complex and interesting redstone devices that allow the player to complete a simple challenge. These minigames can be ones of your own invention, though many builders like to imitate classic board games or arcade games in Minecraft.

For example, Figure 10-5 shows a re-creation of a classic game: Place the objects in the correct slots within a time limit. When players press the button to start the game, they're given 16 different colors of wool blocks and must throw them into the corresponding hoppers before TNT destroys the platform.

This minigame is relatively small, in programming terms, but as with all machines, you need to understand its primary inputs and outputs in order to build it. This list describes the components of this minigame:

- ✓ **A button that starts a timer and provides the player with wool blocks:** I used command blocks for the wool, but dispensers work as well.

- ✓ **A set of hoppers that accepts wool of certain colors and can tell when a single extra block is added to its storage space.** Each hopper on the platform has a second one underneath it, filled with wool of a particular color (so that only wool of this sort can be filtered into it).

- ✓ **A system that checks the contents of every hopper after the timer runs out.** Because there is little room to work with the actual programming, the engineer must use an alternative form of redstone engineering for this task: minecart tracks (as described in Chapter 3). After the timer goes off, TNT minecarts are sent down each of the four tracks and explode only if the player has lost. Thus, for each hopper that is filled, some booster rails are powered and an activator rail is depowered — if all hoppers are filled, the minecarts pass through harmlessly. This combination of minecart tracks and redstone dust allows you to program in a small space without letting the code interfere with itself.

Figure 10-5: A minigame (top) and its inner workings (bottom).

This example shows the process behind designing a minigame. When you create your own minigame, apply these tips:

✔ **Remember what information must be stored in the game.** For example, the game of tic-tac-toe uses nine squares to accept three values (X, O, or blank). In Pong, the game must know the position of the paddles, the scores on each side, and the position and direction of the ball.

These values can be recorded by using entities such as players and minecarts, scoreboard objectives, or huge clusters of memory latches. Just be sure to use a method that can connect smoothly with the rest of your game. This is entirely possible — veteran Minecraft designers have built these games and much more with redstone and command blocks.

⯈ **Connect the player's input to this information.** Think about how each player's actions change the game, from flipping levers to defeating enemies. The player must somehow be able to make his moves, adjust his pieces, and play some part in winning the game. Thus, at least some of your game's stored information has to be hooked up to whichever devices are under the player's control.

⯈ **Attach the stored information to an output, which updates when needed.** For example, if you have a variable that tells you whether a level is complete, you should connect the variable to a device that advances the level when powered.

Constructing an adventure

Designing an adventure is similar to building a minigame, in that the most important element is structure. The structure of an adventure determines where players have to go, what variables govern the players and the environment, and the progression of challenges and rewards.

Figure 10-6 shows a room in an adventure game that effectively challenges, rewards, and progresses the players. When the room is opened, a zombie appears, holding a customized emerald which acts as a key. When the key is placed into a hopper, a checkpoint is unlocked elsewhere, and the door to the next room opens.

Entities and blocks can have special data tags that give them useful features for custom maps. See Chapter 8 to read about these tags and see how to implement them.

This structure employs the following concepts:

- **A challenge-goal relationship:** Players can continue only if they get the key from the zombie, thus requiring them to defeat the zombie. The hopper system makes the goal of the adventure dependent on this particular challenge, a concept that's quite useful in all adventure maps. For example, in a puzzle map, the door might be locked by a lever at the end of a maze.

- **Connections between rooms:** The link between the hopper and the aforementioned checkpoint is an example of rooms that truly affect each other. Some adventure maps make use of this quite often, filling the space between rooms with redstone webs. However, if you do something like this, you must have a concrete idea of your map's floor plan.

- **A simple, small-room setting:** If this adventure map were set outdoors, it might be more difficult to guide players wherever you want them to go. Remember that you can always use iron doors to restrict and lead players, but you can also use items such as pits, mountain ranges, and the tp command.

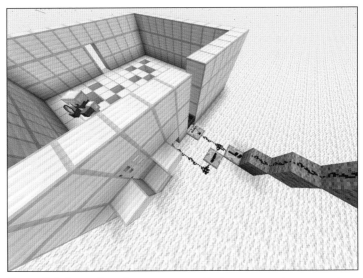

Figure 10-6: A complex adventure room, with the programming exposed. Other, nearby rooms are not shown.

11

Ten Redstone Tricks for Survival Mode

In This Chapter

▸ Interesting methods for improving your survival world

▸ Making your world more efficient and automatic

▸ Making unique additions to your buildings

*T*hough other chapters in this book lay out all the concepts and possibilities of redstone programming, this chapter focuses on ideas for how you can apply them — specifically, in Survival mode. I discuss ten ideas for using redstone that you may find particularly useful or interesting.

Self-Harvesting Farms

As I mention in earlier chapters, many farms can be *self-harvesting* — automated to produce items with little to no input from you. In a game where no resource is permanent, a constant source of items is one of the most permanent ways to make progress in the game.

Figure 11-1 shows two examples of automatic wheat farms using redstone circuitry — one of the farms (top figure) requires bone meal and works much faster; the other (bottom figure) can function on its own.

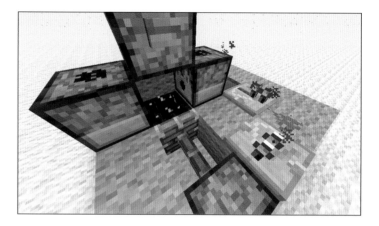

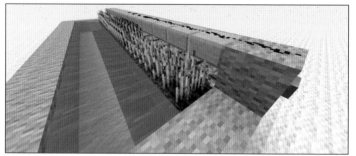

Figure 11-1: Growing and farming wheat with a redstone circuit.

To build these farms, all you have to do is copy the designs shown in Figure 11-1. (You can also work them out yourself or find more designs online.) In the first design, be sure to place a redstone torch on the back of the rightmost dispenser (partly hidden in the figure). Also be sure to use sticky pistons in both designs.

Adjustable Implements

Sometimes you can use automatic functions to make your manual functions more efficient. For example, if you connect a bunch of furnaces with hoppers, you can put items into one of the furnaces, and that furnace will spread the work among all of them. Figure 11-2 shows another idea: If you hook up pistons to the bookcases around your enchanting table, you can improve the table's enchantments whenever you want, and you can remove the bookcases quickly whenever you just want to give an item a simple enchantment.

Figure 11-2: An adjustable enchantment table.

Dungeon Farms

If you encounter a dungeon, don't destroy the mob spawner at its center! This spawner represents an infinite supply of monsters and, consequently, an infinite supply of items. A *dungeon farm* is a machine, often requiring little to no redstone circuitry, that automatically destroys these mobs and salvages their items for you.

You can destroy mobs automatically, if you

- Make them fall a long distance.
- Move them near lava.
- Place them near iron golems.
- Use a piston to push a block over their heads.
- Submerge them in water for a long time.

To do this, surround the spawner with deep pits, iron golems, tanks of water, or whatever else you need. Draining a mob's health is fairly intuitive, but if you're having any trouble, tons of designs are available online to help you out.

Dungeon farms are particularly useful when obtaining blaze rods — these items can be obtained only from the blaze mob, which you can find via mob spawners. Though Blaze cannot be destroyed by falling or burning, be sure to make the most of any blaze spawners you find. (They appear only in nether fortresses, which are often elusive.) Similarly, the End dimension contains plenty of endermen, which you can safely farm after defeating the enderdragon.

You can make a mob farm in another way. It's slower, but you don't need a dungeon for it. All you have to do is build a giant room with the proper conditions for mobs to spawn (for example, build it underground with no lighting to summon night mobs such as zombies). Then you can build the farm around that room, using the same tactics as with a dungeon spawner.

Farm experience orbs, which drop from almost all mobs. These orbs, however, drop only if you strike the final blow yourself. Thus, in order to farm orbs, send mobs down a drop that brings them to a very low health level without destroying them. (The length of this drop depends on the mob.) If you contain the mobs at the bottom of this farm, you can destroy them all in one hit to obtain a massive amount of experience in a short time.

Fast Transportation

Why walk everywhere? Build minecart tracks between your house, your mine, and wherever else you venture. You can use redstone circuitry to automatically load a minecart and change the tracks. You can even send storage minecarts along the track to transport items. Figure 11-3 shows an example of this type of system.

Figure 11-3: A minecart railroad.

 Minecarts act like entities, so they can be destroyed by physical damage. If you create a machine that destroys minecarts on arrival, and place a hopper underneath, you can reload your minecart system automatically by turning the minecart into an item and storing it beneath the tracks. Just don't destroy the item by mistake!

 If you want to send unmanned minecarts along your railroad, keep in mind that a minecart moves faster when a player is inside. You may want to test your track with an unmanned cart to make sure that it can progress all the way without stopping.

Defense Mechanisms

Defense mechanisms are fun, advanced ways to protect yourself and your home. Raise walls around your base at night, create traps that drop the undead into deep chasms, or automatically place blocks in front of your wooden doors whenever you flip a lever. Items such as daylight detectors and pistons are useful in defending your home with style.

You can also use machines to assist you in your nightly ventures. A simple pressure plate surrounded by open doors can trap any mob you lure in, and some well-placed levers can allow you to activate nearby traps if you want to *capture* certain mobs rather than destroy them. Remember, though: Every hostile mob disappears after a while, unless it has been named with the Name Tag item or is carrying one of your items.

Mechanical Lights, Walls, Bridges, and Other Elements

Though some machines make your Minecraft life easier and more automatic, others can make your home more dynamic — or at least more interesting. Cover dark areas with redstone lamps to use as mechanical lights, create walls with collapse to reveal chests and crafting stations, or make bridges that rise from pools of lava, for example. You can do a lot of interesting things with blocks that receive redstone power, especially pistons.

If you want to do something like this, you can hide some redstone circuitry under the ground, over the ceiling, or behind the walls. Remember that you can transmit power through walls by powering blocks (see Chapter 2). Some creative engineering can allow you to power many items inside a room while keeping the circuitry hidden.

Elevators

Elevators can be tricky, requiring you to move the same block up and down over a large distance. Fortunately, simpler versions can move a player vertically with relative ease. These can include pushing stairs into the player's feet to move him upward or alternating between pushing the player upward and moving him to the side. However, one of the simplest techniques — and one of the most entertaining — is the slime block elevator.

Figure 11-4 shows this concept in action. Essentially, this device is meant to send the player from the slime blocks below to the platform above. The player can flip the lever to open the ceiling (pulling apart the four blocks between the pistons), launch herself through it with the slime blocks, and then close the ceiling again in order to land on the floor above. This concept can be expanded in multiple ways: The ceiling might contain slime blocks that launch the player even farther, or the player might be launched sideways over walls.

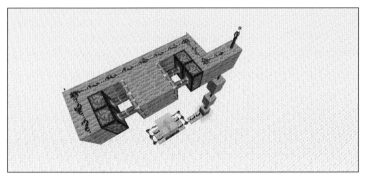

Figure 11-4: An elevator made of slime blocks and a few pistons.

Handy Dispensers

Sorting through chests can be a pain, so it's often helpful to put your most commonly needed items into a dispenser or a dropper. If you stand right next to a dispenser filled with armor, it automatically equips you; similarly, you can use a dropper to hand you your battle gear.

Automatic Notifications

Use daylight sensors, comparators, and other observant devices to tell you exactly what's going on — for example, what the time is or whether your steak has finished cooking. Redstone lamps and note blocks are useful in this regard.

Redstone in Battle

When facing a traditional Minecraft mob, applying redstone in a battle can often be needlessly extravagant. However, if you manage to make an enemy out of another player (many Minecraft servers tend to pit certain players against each other), some of these techniques can be useful.

Figure 11-5 shows three interesting ways to use redstone against your opponents:

- A trap based on a block update detector that ignites a cluster of TNT whenever someone opens the door. This is nothing more than a block update detector, which you can see how to build in Chapter 5.

- A modification on the classic TNT cannon, which fires waves of explosives at the target. Build your own by copying the figure and filling all the dispensers with TNT, or look at some of the many designs online. Also see Chapter 3 for a simple example of a TNT cannon.

- A 12-block-long bridge that lets you build outward without making yourself vulnerable to enemies with ranged attacks. All you need is a piston, a means of powering it (like a pressure plate), and a bunch of blocks for building a barricade.

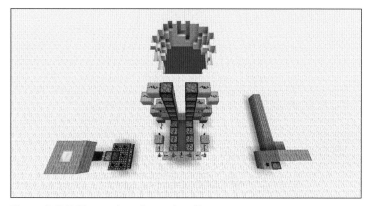

Figure 11-5: Taking engineering to the offense.

Index

About the Author

Jacob Cordeiro is a senior at the Stanford Online High School, and the writer of *Minecraft For Dummies,* Portable Edition and *Gamestar Mechanic For Dummies.* Jacob was a panelist at the ninth annual Games for Change conference, and has a passion for mathematics and game design.

Dedication

To my family and friends. You have all been great navigators, advisors, and peers.

Author's Acknowledgments

Thanks to Amy Fandrei, Kim Darosett, and Becky Whitney, the skilled editors who helped me make each of my books complete.

Thanks to the Nelson family for being excellent friends and technical editors.

Thanks to all of my instructors who taught me the skills that went into this book, including Theodore Alper from Stanford OHS, and Terry Kaufman and Edward Martin from the eIMACS online courses.

Thanks to the vast Minecraft community, which has constantly shown me new and fascinating ideas over the years.

Lastly, thanks to my parents — my mother, whose continuous support provided me with the skills and resources to complete this project, and my father, who gave me every possible opportunity to discover my values and potential.

Publisher's Acknowledgments

Acquisitions Editor: Amy Fandrei

Senior Project Editor: Kim Darosett

Copy Editor: Becky Whitney

Technical Editor: Ryan W. Nelson

Editorial Assistant: Claire Johnson

Sr. Editorial Assistant: Cherie Case

Project Coordinator: Erin Zeltner

Cover Photo: Cover image courtesy of Jacob Cordeiro